LITSA I. HATZIFOTI
Archaeologist

Minoan Crete

EDITIONS M. TOUBIS S.A.

© Copyright 2005   MICHAEL TOUBIS EDITIONS S.A.
                     Nisiza Karela, Koropi, Attiki
                     Telephone: +30 210 6029974, Fax: +30 210 6646856
                     Web Site: http://www.toubis.gr

ISBN: 960-540-575-X

Rhyton of black
serpentite stone
in the shape of a bull's
head, from the palace
of Knossos. The bull
was the Minoans'
sacred animal
and the bull's head
was a sacred symbol
of their cult.
(1700-1450 BC,
Archaeological
Museum of Herakleio).

Contents

*T*oday's travellers to Crete who love its history and monuments will need to put in a lot of time before they can say they have seen Crete in all the manifestations of its culture.

It is a place in which a great many elements of European civilisation appear for the first time, with architectural monuments that are unique in area, volume, wealth and history; international trade relations with all the known peoples of the world at that time, especially ancient Egypt, where there is abundant evidence of the Keftiu who have been identified as Cretans; a religion manifest in every expression of daily life; love of nature confirmed, inter alia, by the presence of the plant, marine and animal worlds in works of art; respect for the human being demonstrated by the attention to and care of the dead in magnificent necropolises; and above all their singular art, whose duration is long and multifaceted. It is a place, then, whose myths, tradition, and high level of culture attract and charm anyone who decides to investigate it.

The culture of Crete is splendid at every period. But anyone who studies it in an effort to capture it as an overall mental concept will fail.

The pages that follow aim to give a simple but informative picture of the singular Minoan civilisation that developed on this island, by providing visitors with detailed descriptions of monuments and works of art, with a view to introducing them to its spirit and inspiring them to become better acquainted with the achievements of people who lived millennia earlier and have bequeathed us sublime and incomparable works.

Time chart

To help readers understand the various chronological references in the descriptions of Minoan monuments and works of art, we are providing here a simplified time chart with the main chronological designations used by Minoan scholars.

There are, of course, other charts with further sub-divisions, but we believe that the ordinary reader who wants a general picture of the period would not be particularly interested in the special chronological designations useful to people who are systematically engaged in studying the era of the Minoan civilisation. It is worth noting that the parallel study of the Egyptian and Minoan civilisations has been of great assistance in establishing the absolute dating of the latter through their contemporary artefacts.

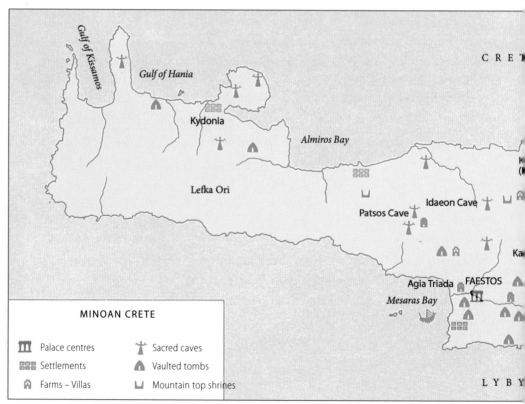

CRET

Gulf of Kissamos

Gulf of Hania

Kydonia

Almiros Bay

Lefka Ori

Patsos Cave

Idaeon Cave

Agia Triada   FAESTOS

Mesaras Bay

Ka

LYBY

MINOAN CRETE

	Palace centres		Sacred caves
	Settlements		Vaulted tombs
	Farms – Villas		Mountain top shrines

5000 – 2600 BC	Neolithic Age
2600 – 2000 BC	Prepalatial Period
2000 – 1700 BC	Protopalatial Period
1700 – 1400 BC	Neopalatial Period
1400 – 1100 BC	Postpalatial Period
1100 – 900 BC	Protogeometric Period
900 – 725 BC	Geometric Period
725 – 650 BC	Orientalising Period
650 – 500 BC	Archaic Period
500 – 330 BC	Classical Period
330 – 67 BC	Hellenistic Period
67 BC – 323AD	Greco-Roman Period

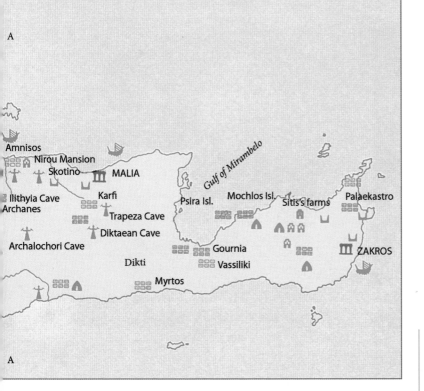

Map showing the Minoan monuments of Crete.

The Throne Room at the palace of Knossos.
A copy of the wall painting with griffins decorates the walls.

The Crete of Minos

- ◆ The Island of Myths
- ◆ The Minoan Civilisation

Chapter 1

The Crete of Minos

Amidst the wine-dark sea lies Crete,
a fair rich island populous beyond compute,
with ninety cities of mixed speech, where several languages
co-exist. Besides the Cretans proper there are Achaeans,
Cydonians, Dorians of tossing crest and noble Pelasgians.
The capital is Knossos, ruled by Minos
who from his ninth year talked familiarly with great Zeus.

Odyssey, Book 19.
Translated by T.E. Lawrence,
Wordsworth Editions Ltd. 1992.

Homer described Crete in these words, echoing through myths a greatness that he himself could never have imagined. Everything that today comprises the civilisation created in Crete during the pre-historic period – an enormous number of buildings, cemeteries, works of art and household utensils, its religion, trade relations and cultural exchanges – is known by the name derived from its famous King Minos.

The Island of Myths

Son of Zeus and Europa, brother of Rhadamanthys and Sarpedon, Minos had four sons and four daughters by Pasiphaë, daughter of Helios and Persa and sister of Aeëtes and Circe. One of their daughters was Ariadne. Poseidon gave Minos a beautiful bull to be sacrificed, but Minos sacrificed another in its place, and to punish him the god caused Pasiphaë to fall madly in love with the bull. From their union a monster was born with the head of a bull and a man's body who fed on human flesh. He was called Asterion but became known as the Minotaur. He lived hidden in the Labyrinth, a dark, underground place with endless corridors that nobody who entered could hope to get out of alive. The Minotaur was destroyed by Theseus. He found his way out with the help of the ball of thread given to him by Ariadne, who had fallen in love with him. They left for Athens together, but Theseus abandoned her on the island of Naxos.

A great deal of time would be required to unravel the myths associated with Minos and his family. A great deal of effort would likewise be required, and perhaps ultimately in vain, to sweep away the mists surrounding this figure and to determine whether he ever actually existed or whether this name was just a title.

In any event, what is concentrated in his name is the power and radiance of the civilisation that existed in Crete for centuries and became known among all the peoples of the Mediterranean, and which even today the whole world admires and respects. Because Minos not only built cities, roads and ports, he not only placed Talus – the last man of the ancient bronze race, not dissimilar to today's robots – to guard the island's coasts, he not only built ships, and not only travelled to distant ports. He was, in addition, a man famed for his justice, who every nine years would ascend Mount Ida, to a cave in which he would meet his father, who gave him the wise laws with which he governed and judged his people.

Tradition says that he died a terrible death in Sicily. He was killed so that he would not be able to punish the architect Daedalus whom he was pursuing. Herakleia Minoa was founded on the spot where he died. Later other cities were built with the same name, evidence of the Minoans' commercial and naval activity.

"Theseus kills the Minotaur", representation of the myth of the Minotaur on an Attic black-figure amphora. Below, detail of the scene (c. 540 BC, Louvre Museum, Paris).

Minoan Civilisation

We have no information from written sources about the Minoan Civilisation that developed on Crete during the prehistoric period. Everything we know, apart from myths, has been revealed to us, sometimes gradually and sometimes suddenly, by archaeological excavations, which had frequently been preceded by curiosity and greed, ignorance and indifference. The artefacts that have been unearthed and preserved are waiting for others to come to light that will supplement the picture of the life and achievements of these people who bequeathed us a great deal and who, as one scholar of antiquity has noted, lived better than anybody else in Europe sixteen centuries before Christ. At the same time these artefacts constitute living testimony to an art that brims over with originality, attesting to a very special culture.

The changes that occurred over the centuries were manifested in the first large palaces in central and particularly in eastern Crete (Knossos, Phaistos, Mallia, Zakros, Archanes). These unfortified palaces and other buildings were totally destroyed around 1700 BC, but were very soon rebuilt: larg-

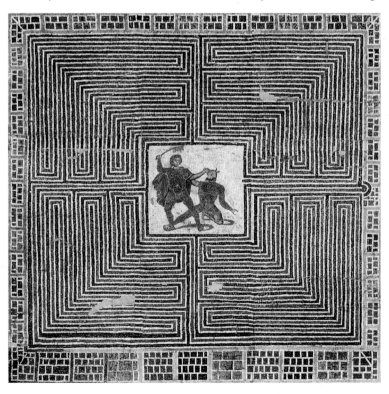

Theseus and the Minotaur in the Labyrinth, marble Roman mosaic (4th cent. AD, History of Art Museum, Vienna).

Opposite page: "The fall of Icarus", relief from Roman sarcophagus (mid 2nd cent. AD, National Museum of Messene).

er, more complex and with more floors, gathering on their premises not only accommodations, i.e. the residence of their owners, but also baths, many shrines and sanctuaries, enormous storage areas for liquid (oil, wine) and dry foodstuffs (grains, pulses, etc.), administration quarters, luxurious reception halls, workshops, archive rooms, balconies overlooking the superb natural environment, many doors, light wells, and treasuries. All these are laid out around a central court on a north-south axis, while on the west side there is another court of indeterminate shape, in which there is frequently a stepped structure designated as a "theatre" and associated with presentations, ceremonies or games of a religious-cult nature. Columns, piers, vivid colours and wall paintings with ritual themes, sacred symbols or scenes from the realm of nature provide a bright, cheerful atmosphere that appears to have pervaded the life of the Minoans, keeping the fear of death at a distance. A great variety of religious rites were carried out in a festive atmosphere with many naturalist elements such as trees, miscellaneous animals etc., symbolising the presence of the god, and depicted in various works of art.

Over the centuries, the size and complexity of Minoan palaces gave rise to the myth of the Labyrinth, which was undoubtedly related not only to the dimensions of the building but also to the power of the Minoan state. At the same time the memory of the Minotaur has been perpetuated by bull-vaulting and athletic contests with bulls that are frequently represented on wall paintings and other works of art.

The "Blue Ladies" wall painting from the palace of Knossos.

Minoan Art

- ◆ Pottery
- ◆ Stone carving
- ◆ Miniature sculpture
- ◆ Sealstone carving
- ◆ Gold work and Jewellery
- ◆ Painting

Chapter 2

Minoan Art

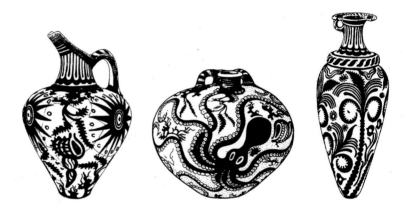

Typical shapes
of Minoan pottery:
prochous (ewer)
with a beaked spout,
round flask and
conic rhyton.

Opposite page:
Kamares ware krater
with applied white
clay lilies
from Phaistos
(1850-1750 BC,
Archaeological
Museum
of Herakleio).

Art is the way in which the aesthetic, religious and cultural quests of a people are expressed; it is a function not only of their skills but also of many other factors, such as the environment, social, political and economic conditions, the available materials, technical knowledge and the influences of neighbouring peoples. In the case of prehistoric Crete, art was, like the palaces, an expression of the civilisation of the people who inhabited the island.

At different periods, this art was expressed in works of unparalleled beauty in the arts of ceramics, pottery-painting, gold and metalwork, stone carving, sealstone carving, sculpture and painting. Although their dimensions were usually in inverse proportion to the palaces, because no large-scale objects (statues, etc.) have been found, in terms of artistic and technical merit they are unrivalled.

Pottery

Ceramics and pottery painting, crafts which have been practised by man since the dawn of time, go back in Crete as far as the Neolithic age. We also have significant examples from the Prepalatial period. They are found primarily as funeral gifts in graves.

During this period, in the region in which the earliest examples were found, one can distinguish the so-called "Pyrgos" style of pottery with a monochrome, black, grey or chestnut-coloured surface, the "Ayios Onoufrios" style with brown linear decoration on a lighter ground, the polychrome "Royal" style created by deliberately non-uniform baking, and the "white" style which comprised white decoration on a black surface.

During the Protopalatial period, the pottery known as Kamares ware was foremost; it was produced in Knossos and Phaistos and is distinguishable for its superb quality (some have such thin walls that they constitute the eggshell subcategory) and polychrome painted decoration in exquisite designs with bands, rosettes, hatching, spirals etc. and some-

1. Prochous with long, beak-shaped spout and linear decoration in the "white" style, from Mochlos (2500-1900 BC, Archaeological Museum of Herakleio).

2. Prochous in the "Ayios Onouphrios" style (2500-1900 BC, Archaeological Museum of Herakleio).

3. Prochous with beaked spout and dotted decoration in the "royal" style (2500-2200 BC, Archaeological Museum of Herakleio).

times applied decorative relief motifs (flowers etc.). At the same period, there were also the pots of the "barbotine" type which, in addition to being painted, were also covered with spiky relief decoration.

In the Neopalatial period that followed, the strong naturalistic mood that appeared in the Kamares ware evolved into the flower vases and marine ware which, instead of abstract patterns, depicted plants and animals from the marine world. Octopus, nautiluses, starfish, murex, papyrus, lilies and irises testify to an uninhibited artistic imagination and skill that created works of extraordinary variety and beauty.

Cups, ewers *(prochooi)*, cylindrical vases with lid *(pyxides)*, "teapots", "fruit stands", drinking cups *(skyphoi)*, cooking pans *(lopades)*, small and large storage jars *(pitharia)*, and bowls for mixing wines *(krateres)* are the most frequently encountered types of pottery. Some have been so well wrought and preserved that they would be admired by the very best practitioners of the trade today as works of sublime artistry.

The Neopalatial period boasts yet another highlight in the realm of ceramics that can be seen in stunning examples of the "palace" style, and come solely from the Palace of

Prochous with polychrome spiky relief decoration in the "barbotine" style, from the vaulted tomb of Mesara (2100-1900 BC, Archaeological Museum of Herakleio).

Knossos. On them, the naturalistic decoration has been disciplined into geometric schematisation, without any limitation being imposed on the imagination, in terms of the magnificence or variety of the curved designs. The well-known old types of pottery now included false-mouthed amphorae.

1. Earthenware ritual prochous of the "palace" style from the Katsabas grave (1450-1400 BC, Archaeological Museum of Herakleio).

2. Conic rhyton decorated with starfish, nautiluses etc. in the "marine" style from the palace at Zakros (c. 1500 BC, Archaeological Museum of Herakleio).

3. Spherical prochous with beaked spout and representations of aquatic birds (1700-1400 BC, Archaeological Museum of Herakleio).

4. Earthenware flask in the marine style decorated with octopus, from Palaikastro (c. 1500 BC, Archaeological Museum of Herakleio).

5. Kamares ware pithos-type pot decorated with palm trees, from Knossos (c. 1700 BC, Archaeological Museum of Herakleio).

2

3

4

5

1. The "vessel of the reapers" in black serpentine stone. From the villa at Ayia Triada (1550-1500 BC, Archaeological Museum of Herakleio).

2. The "presentation cup" or "cup of the leader", in black serpentine stone with relief decoration. From the villa at Ayia Triada (1550-1500 BC, Archaeological Museum of Herakleio).

Stone carving

The existence of multicoloured stone such as marble, alabaster, steatite and basalt etc. created the conditions required for the development of stone carving in Minoan Crete. Although this art was taught by the people of the Cyclades and Egypt – the presence of many Cycladic figurines and stone objects of Egyptian origin in graves in many different regions testifies to this – the pupils surpassed their teachers. Utilising the chromatic varieties of the veined rock and their bold imagination, they created superb works of art in terms of both technique and design. Among the stone ritual vessels in particular, certain relief pots occupy a special place in Minoan art. Their importance lies in their skilled decoration with lively relief scenes from the life and the habits of the Minoans in compositions with many figures. Typical examples are the three serpentite rhyta from Ayia Triada representing a procession of threshers, scenes of wrestling, boxing and bull-vaulting (athletics with bulls) and figures of young warriors, as well as a rhyton depicting a mountain top sanctuary in chlorite stone with applied gold from the palace of Zakros.

The skill of the stone-carvers can also be seen on rhyta in the shape of animal heads (bull from Zakros and Knossos, lioness from Knossos).

In addition to stone carving, the Minoans created other sculptured works from different materials, but they did not produce works of large dimensions, despite their frequent contacts with Egypt and their knowledge of its colossal statuary. Large-scale sculptures might, of course, have existed; but if they had been made of corruptible materials like wood, stucco and soft limestone, they would have not been preserved.

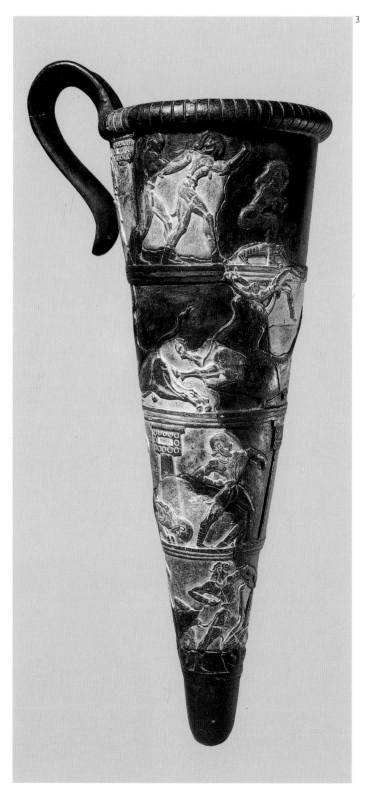

3. Conic rhyton
of black serpentite
stone with four relief
scenes. From top
to bottom: wrestling,
boxing and
bull-vaulting.
From the villa
at Ayia Triada
(1550-1500 BC,
Archaeological
Museum
of Herakleio).

4. Rhyton of rock
crystal, bronze
on the handle
and gold on the neck.
From the palace
of Zakros
(c. 1500 BC,
Archaeological
Museum
of Herakleio).

1. Figurine of the "Great Goddess of the Snakes", faience. From the palace of Knossos (c. 1600 BC, Archaeological Museum of Herakleio).

2. Group of female figures dancing around a musician playing the lyre. From Palaikastro (1350-1110 BC, Archaeological Museum of Herakleio).

3. Earthenware figurine of a goddess with a crown of doves. One of the goddess of Gazi (1400-1150 BC, Archaeological Museum of Herakleio).

Miniature sculpture

Miniature sculpture, especially in the period between 1600-1450 BC, presents many exceptional figurines of male votaries of a divinity to whom they were dedicated. Snake goddesses in faience and miscellaneous figurines in stone, clay or ivory constitute characteristic examples of Minoan miniature sculpture. Clay figurines depict individual persons or animals, such as the goddesses of Gazi, or groups such as the clay replicas of dancing and the worship of the dead from Kamilari. Also a group of female figures holding each other's shoulders dance around a musician standing in the middle, from Palaikastro.

It is worth reiterating here that Cretan art, which was primarily devoted to painting, did not produce large-scale works of sculpture.

Earthenware replica of a small circular shrine (1100-1000 BC, Yamalakis Collection, Archaeological Museum of Herakleio).

1. Gold seal ring with
the representation of a sacred
religious dance. From the tomb
of the Isopati near Knossos
(1500 BC, Archaeological Museum
of Herakleio).

2. Chalcedony sealstone set in gold,
representing a hunting scene
(1500 BC, Archaeological Museum
of Herakleio).

3. Lentoid sealstone
of turquoise set in gold,
representing a hunting scene
(1600-1100 BC, Archaeological
Museum of Herakleio).

Sealstone carving

At all phases of Minoan civilisation, the crafts-men's ability to represent figures on hard material and on a surface of minimal dimensions is demonstrated in sealstone carving. Agate, amethyst, jasper, turquoise, steatite, sardonyx, chalcedony, hematite, sard, faience, and rock crystal are some of the semi-precious materials on which artists used their skill and imagination to carve scenes from rituals, bullfights, and bull-vaulting, as well as figures of people (infrequently), animals, and mythical figures with great precision. These compositions have been adapted to the surface of the seal in such a way as to radiate elegance, vitality, movement and sensitivity, adding to the evidence of a high cultural and artistic level.

In Crete, artisans did not follow blindly the Eastern models of carving sealstones, but took the art a step further by creating compositions using parts of different scenes, irrespective of their subject matter, based on strictly aesthetic criteria.

Visitors to the Archaeological Museum of Herakleio and the other Cretan museums who devote some time and attention to examining these sealstones have much to enjoy and gain from these miniature works of art, which reveal the power and skill of those who created the Minoan civilisation. As a scholar of Cretan culture has observed, sealstone carving is the pre-eminent art of the Cretans, as it combines the unexpected, original, outstanding and mysterious; in other words it looks forward to what is commonly called poetry, which is not an exaggeration.

Gold work and Jewellery

Cretan art was so highly developed that it naturally influenced the goldsmith's and jeweller's arts. We have already seen that the Minoans were superb craftsmen in creating miniature works of art. During the Protopalatial period, together with the foundation of the palaces, there was a gradual shift in Minoan society: the further specialisation of trades created social classes with stricter dividing lines between them. Precious metals, which were largely imported from Egypt and the East, were used to lend luxury, at the same time reinforcing the social stratification. Gold jewellery in particular has been discovered as funeral gifts (Mochlos, Mesara, Chrysolakkos near Mallia, etc.), among which is the characteristic pendant with the two facing bees holding a piece of honeycomb.

More finds from the Neopalatial period have been discovered: rings with and without seals, amulets, necklaces, brooches, etc. It can be concluded from the high aesthetic level and superb workmanship that the Minoans also excelled in this expression of artistic creation, by means of which art became part of their daily lives.

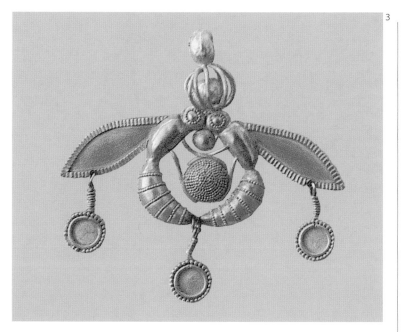

1. Gold earring in the shape of a bull's head from the Trapeza site (14th-13th cent. BC, Archaeological Museum of Herakleio).

2. Gold heart-shaped amulet with relief decoration. From Ayia Triada (14th-12th cent. BC, Archaeological Museum of Herakleio).

3. Gold jewel in the form of two bees holding a piece of honeycomb, from the palace of Mallia (16th-14th cent. BC, Archaeological Museum of Herakleio).

Painting

Another important domain of Minoan artistic expression can be seen in the wall paintings that have been brought to light in the palaces and villas. Even though only a small part of the total has been preserved, it is enough to give us an idea of the main features of this art and of its genuine expression.

What is striking on Minoan wall paintings is the artists' preference for themes with animals and plants, as well as ceremonies or processions of supplication to the divine to ensure that nature would blossom and bear fruit, i.e. for fertility to be perpetuated. The artists used colours and two dimensions to serve the proper decoration of the palace or other area that they were painting, and created images of harmony and beauty.

1. "The wall painting of the lilies", sample of the wonderful wall paintings in the Villa of the Lilies in ancient Amnisos (c. 1500 BC, Archaeological Museum of Herakleio),

2. "The Dancer" part of a wall painting (c. 1450 BC, Archaeological Museum of Herakleio).

3. "The Prince with the lilies" part of a wall painting from the palace of Knossos (c. 1550 BC, Archaeological Museum of Herakleio).

3

In about 1600 BC, a few works were created in which the figures were shaped with plaster in such a way as to render them in low relief, and were then painted to make them livelier. This category includes the so-called "Prince of the lilies" from the Palace of Knossos, the "Seated goddess" from Pseira, and the olives from Knossos. Some of the themes of wall paintings that have been preserved and are now exhibited in the Herakleio Museum include religious scenes with processions of slender youths, bull-vaulting, the sacred forest, the "Parisienne" (a wonderful female figure), griffins, dolphins, eight-shaped shields, lilies, marine landscapes, and the famous "Crocus-gatherer", all constitute superb expressions of Minoan art.

Another splendid example of Minoan painting is on the unique sarcophagus found at Ayia Triada, which will be discussed separately below.

It is worth noting that Minoan painting does not seek to imitate the exterior environment. Artists attempted to render themes from their own point of view, serving purposes that were mainly architectural; in this way, their main effort was to show up the buildings.

This view of the decorative purpose of Minoan painting is corroborated by the framing of the wall paintings in most cases with parallel bands of bright colour. The prevailing subject matter, as we have seen, usually consists of scenes from daily life, religious scenes and themes from nature, among which a special place is held by renderings of spring landscapes and the marine world.

Wall painting with partridges from the Caravanserai in the palace of Knossos (16th cent. BC, Archaeological Museum of Herakleio).

"The Parisienne" part of a wall painting from Knossos (c. 1450 BC, Archaeological Museum of Herakleio).

Minoan painting follows the strict canons of the Egyptian tradition. Figures are usually rendered in profile, with the eye depicted frontally, as can be seen below.

Bull-vaulting. Wall painting from the palace of Knossos
(16th cent. BC, Archaeological Museum of Herakleio).

"The blue bird", part of the decoration in the "House of Frescoes". From the palace of Knossos (c. 1550 BC, Archaeological Museum of Herakleio).

Below: Painted reproduction of the wall painting with the "blue bird"(drawn by G. Angelinis).

Minoan culture, then, led artistic expression onto new, un-charted paths; utilising every favourable feature – including the island's geographical location, the exchange of cultural el-ements with other peoples, and the absence of a direct hostile threat – it poroduced magnificent works that were to exert a catalytic influence on the evolution of Greek art. The great flourishing of the arts in Minoan Crete was not a historic fact alone or an isolated chapter in art history. Even though the Minoan civilisation developed in an age far removed from our own, its characteristic features,, such as peace, justice, joy and light, the worship of nature and the artistic disposition that brim over with refinement and poetic roots into every sector of daily life are strongly manifest in the examples that have been preserved. This culture has had a major influence on world civilisation because, linked as it is with nature and fertility, it constitutes the best expression of respect for Crea-tion, and modern ecological movements would have much to gain by drawing from its deeper messages.

Detail from the decoration of the poros stone sarcophagus of Ayia Triada, with representations
of Minoan funeral rites. Priestesses remove the blood of the bull after its sacrifice and priests offer animals
(c. 1400 BC, Archaeological Museum of Herakleio).

The Minoan Religion

Chapter 3

The Minoan Religion

Earthenware figurine of a "kourotrophos" goddess who is holding the "divine infant" high in her arms. From the palace of Knossos 1450-1300 BC, Archaeological Museum of Herakleio).

The direct relationship of the inhabitants of Minoan Crete with nature, seasonal changes, weather phenomena, and the germination, flowering, harvest and death in winter of the plant world created forms that personified their joys and sorrows, their hopes and fears.

The basic feature was the personification of nature in a woman – the Great Mother – a figure which can be encountered in the religions of the Eastern peoples under many different names (Cybele, Ishtar, Isis, Aphrodite, etc.) and appeared in various representations (Mountain Mother, Mistress of the Beasts) with animals or holding an infant god (*Kourtrophos*).

The Minoans associated this reproductive power that they identified in nature with a fertilising element, a Divine Infant or Young God, who is united with the Mother Goddess, dies and is resurrected in a manner analogous to the cycle of the seasons and, as noted by the eminent religious scholar M.P. Nilsson, symbolises the spirit of fertility, the new life that begins in spring. There is a similar element in the religions of the East (Attis, Baal, Osiris, Tamuz). He is usually represent-

Opposite page:
The bull occupied
a special position
among the sacred
animals. Stone rhyton
in the shape of a bull's
head, chlorite with
gold-revetted horns.
From the palace
of Zakros
(1700-1400 BC.
Archaeological
Museum
of Herakleio).

Figurine of
the "Small goddess
of the snakes",
faience. Palace
of Knossos
(c. 1600 BC,
Archaeological
Museum
of Herakleio).

ed as a hunter or a tamer of wild beasts, armed with a shield, bow, etc. and accompanied by real or mythical animals (panthers, dogs, griffins, etc.).

Many of the features of these pre-Hellenic deities were handed down to the gods of Olympus, a fact that can be proved by studying the Linear B tablets, both from Knossos and from other regions of Greece, such as Pylos, since the figures on them are not exclusively Minoan.

Very few cult objects from the Protopalatial and Neopalatial periods have been found. On the contrary, a number of idols have been discovered from the Postpalatial period, placed in conspicuous positions in sacred areas, bearing different symbols, with their arms in a variety of positions.

The view has been expressed that in the centuries from which no religious idols have been found, particular persons may have symbolised the divine – the king or members of his family and members of the priesthood – and that they played the part symbolically. Priests can be identified in works of art by their special dress, characteristic robes reminiscent of Eastern models with oblique bands. On the Ayia Triada sarcophagus, priests and priestesses are garbed from the waist down in animal skins that allude to sacrifices. The priesthood offered sacrifices of all kinds, burned incense, conducted exorcisms etc.

Snakes occupy a special position among the other sacred animals such as the bulls, cows, wild goats and doves. Sacred animals may often symbolise the presence of the divinity.

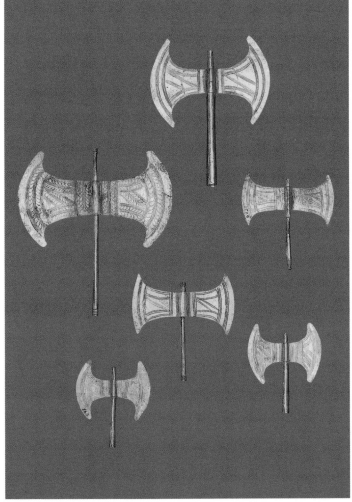

1. The south
Propylaeum of
the palace of Knossos
with the sacred horns.

2. Relief plaque
of faience with
representation
of a wild goat
(c. 1600 BC,
Archaeological
Museum of Herakleio).

3. Votive gold double
axes with incised
decoration. From
the cave of Arkalohori
(1600-1450 BC,
Archaeological
Museum of Herakleio).

The rape of Europa by Zeus, who transformed himself into a bull, certainly echoes this symbolism; birds are added to figures that symbolise gods in order to demonstrate their presence ("epiphany").

A special characteristic of Minoan Crete from the religious viewpoint is the dearth of temples, a fact that differentiates the religion of the Minoans from that of the Egyptians and the Mesopotamians. Many places of worship have been identified in palaces and dwellings; they have no specific external features, but present some particularity in their interior layout. On the contrary, sacred symbols such as the horns, the double axe or the representations painted on walls with symbolic motifs testify that the entire palace is, to one degree or another, a sanctuary.

The Minoan temple at Anemospilia

The only independent temple known to date in Minoan Crete was discovered in 1979 by Mr & Mrs Sakellarakis on the Anemospilia site, on Mt Youchta near Archanes. Built on a small tongue of land, it consists of three oblong rooms with very strong walls that do not communicate among themselves, but are connected on the north side by a corridor that runs along the entire width of the building.

The east room has a stepped altar on its south wall. During the excavations, it was found to contain a large number of pots of various shapes and sizes that were used in blood-

Painted representation of the hall of the double axes (Drawing: Piet de Jong).

less sacrifices. The presence of sea pebbles in this area is distinctive, as it suggests the close relationship of the marine element with the Minoan religion.

The room in the centre was full of large vessels. A piece of natural rock juts out from the south and southwest section, where a bench had been hewn. Near it, among other things, a pair of larger than life-size clay feet was found suggesting the existence of an "acrolith" statue, i.e. the trunk of a tree, on which "garments" were hung, creating a type of *xoano* (cult wooden statue) known from a number of Minoan works of art and from the excavations of analogous religious statues from historic times.

The west room, without significant movable finds, presents architectural asymmetries as well as structures that testify to the use of this area for blood sacrifices. This room in the sacred building at Anemospilia contained features that make it unique in Crete. Excavations there revealed the skeletons of four people, three men and one woman. Two men and the woman were found to have fallen on the floor, according to expert anthropologists and coroners, having died a sudden violent death caused by the fall of construction materials and an intense fire. The fourth man was found on a trapezoidal structure, in a special side position with a bronze weapon over him.

According to archaeologist Giannis Sakellarakis who conducted the excavations, these findings constitute evidence of human sacrifice, which has not been found anywhere else in Crete up to the present day, although it is known from other regions of the Eastern Mediterranean (Egypt, Palestine). The same archaeologist explained the theme of human sacrifice in ancient Greece clearly and with much evidence and information.

Other than the known sacrifice of Iphigenia at Aulis, there are other analogous references and not only from mythological traditions. He also observed that this is not a customary practice, but a desperate action in face of a terrifying event such as an earthquake, in an effort to appease the god, and noted that this sacrifice took place on an isolated and closed site.

The temple at Anemospilia was destroyed during the first half of the 17th century BC, as testified by the famous Kamares ware found in it, and was not used again.

Bronze statuette of a male figure in a stance of respect. From Tylissos (1500 BC, Archaeological Museum of Herakleio).

The sacred caves of Crete

Caves, especially those with impressive stalactites and stalagmites, frequently constituted places of worship for the Minoans, given that Crete has many caves of exceptional interest from all viewpoints. Many Cretan caves functioned for centuries as places of worship, and are now treasuries for archaeological exploration.

In some caves, the religion changed and worship continued there after the advent of Christianity and in many, it continues up to the present time. Some 120 caves are recorded as Christian churches. The best known and most important caves, especially from an archaeological viewpoint, are the following:

◆ The cave of Ilithyia near Amnisos, Herakleio, known from the time of Homer and Strabo. Here, according to legend, Hera gave birth to Ilithyia, the goddess who supported mothers in childbirth.

◆ The cave of Ayia Paraskevi near Skotino, Pediada, 22 km from Herakleio. Archaeologists have identified worship on this site from 1900 BC to the 4th cent. AD. It is a particularly magnificent cave owing to its stalactites and stalagmites. Cult site of the goddess Britomartis (Sweet virgin).

◆ The cave of Arkalohori. Important religious centre from the mid-3rd millennium BC, near Arkalohori. A sword 1,55 m. long, unique of its kind in Europe, was found here, together with other valuable objects that escaped being plundered because part of the cave collapsed a very long time ago.

◆ The Kamares cave. It had been inhabited as early as the Neolithic period and was a place of worship in Minoan times. This cave gave its name to a large number of exquisite pieces of pottery first found in it that had been used by the faithful to carry their offerings. This pottery was produced by workshops in the palaces of Knossos and Phaistos.

◆ The Dictaean Cave, in which Zeus was said to have been born, on the Lasithi plateau. With many stalactites and stalagmites, it was in constant use for religious purposes from 2000 BC until 100 AD and the source of an enormous number of finds, despite predations by illegal excavations.

◆ The Idaean Cave, known as the cave of Psychro, 21 km from Anogia, a place in which, according to a different myth, Zeus was born or raised. It was a significant place of worship

Scarab of white steatite from the Trapeza cave in Lasithi, attests to contacts with Egypt (1530-1400 BC, Archaeological Museum of Herakleio).

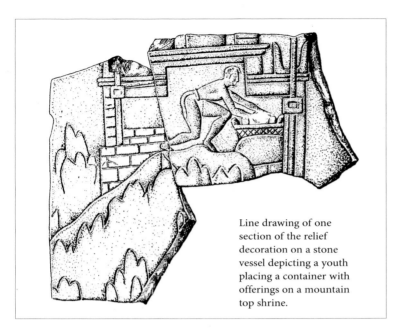

Line drawing of one section of the relief decoration on a stone vessel depicting a youth placing a container with offerings on a mountain top shrine.

in the Minoan period with rich finds and splendid anthropomorphic stalactites.

◆ The cave of Patsos at Amari Rethymnon, a famous sanctuary in which a religious cult began in the Minoan period and continued into historic times, when Cranaeus Hermes was worshipped.

◆ The cave of the Cyclops at Souyia, near Chania. It was thus named because the inside of the cave presented similarities to Homer's description of the cave of the Cyclops.

◆ The Trapeza cave or Kronio near the village of Tzermiado, Lasithi was initially used as a dwelling place and then as a burial ground, with many noteworthy findings among which were scarabs, testifying to contacts with Egypt.

◆ The cave of Ayia Fotini on the road from Herakleio to the Lasithi Plateau was used as a place of worship from about the middle of the 2nd millennium (1550 BC) up to the Roman era and has yielded a wealth of finds.

◆ The cave of Stravomiti on the southwest slopes of Youchta produced finds ranging from the Neolithic period to historic times. It was used at different times as a place for burial, residence and worship. It was dedicated to a female deity.

In addition to caves, mountain peaks were also used as places of worship in the Minoan era. On Youchtas, Petsofas, Prinias, Xirokampos, Profitis Ilias at Mallia, Kalamaki etc., mountain top shrines have been discovered.

Clay figurine of an armed man in a stance of worship. From the mountain top shrine at Petsofas (1950 BC, Archaeological Museum of Herakleio).

Tree worship, widespread among many peoples, including the Teutons, was a significant religious element among the Minoans and is associated with the longevity of certain trees or their contribution to the nutrition and economy of the community, such as the olive tree, and to the sacredness of the column.

As observed by an expert on the Minoan civilisation, the researcher has a strong sense of the diffuse presence of the deity among the Minoan Cretans. In palaces and country houses, decoration including the double axe, sacred horns and other motifs bears witness to the fact that all parts of buildings were cloaked in sacredness. But there were also particular places of worship, such as the "three-part sanctuaries", crypts with a square central pillar, sacred reservoirs or purification areas that were believed to have been baths, but in the absence of drainage at these points, in contrast with the significant sewerage system in the Minoan palaces, this hypothesis does not stand up.

In all these areas, many ritual vessels were found, some of precious materials, as well as tables for offerings, figurines, etc. reinforcing the certainty that they were sacred sites.

Characteristic types of figurines that symbolise the female deity in the earliest period were plastic representations of obese nude women. Later, the nakedness was limited. Suffice it here to refer to the bell-shaped pots that have a link so that they can be hung up, two holes for eyes and horn-like protrusions that symbolise masks, and garments, or they may be votive bells to the snake goddesses, bare-breasted female figures that are richly dressed to symbolise the divinity.

Pithari (large storage jar) with the sacred symbol of the double axe. From the palace of Knossos (c. 1500 BC, Archaeological Museum of Herakleio).

The double axe and the horns have already been mentioned as sacred symbols of the Minoan religion. Here too we should mention the knot, a ribbon tied in such a way as to resemble a bow knot. The knot has a protective significance. The eight-shaped shield, the helmet, the cross in different variations and the wheel were all used for deterrent, defensive and offertory purposes.

In addition to sacrifices of animals, which took place on large altars or other smaller ones to hold offerings, religious artefacts frequently found in the Minoan palaces included offering tables made of stone or clay with special hollows for libations etc. Other characteristic types of objects related to religious worship were the *kernos,* i.e. a vessel for offerings that usually had a large hollow in the middle and many smaller ones around it for offering small amounts of fruit, the *rhyton* for offering liquids, which was in the shape of various animal heads (bull, snake, dog) or even a human one, and other types of vessels found in sacred places.

Worship of the dead seems to have begun towards the end of the Prepalatial period, a fact that is manifested by offerings to the dead not only when they were buried, but also for a long time afterward. The relationship between the living and the dead is depicted on sarcophagi, although it is not clear whether the scenes allude to the sacredness of the dead person or whether the intervention and protection of the god is sought. Indeed in the graves discovered at Fourni, certain practices attest to the worship of the dead. In any event, a characteristic but unique example of a monument of this type is the sarcophagus of Ayia Triada, which is believed to have been the tomb of a financially and socially eminent person.

Ritual prochous with relief representation of a "sacred knot". From the palace of Knossos (1400-1100 BC, Archaeological Museum of Herakleio).

Minoan sarcophagi, including that of Ayia Triada, may strike the viewer as strange because of their very small size, in comparison especially with the tall and gallant bearing of modern Cretans. But as the skeletons found inside sarcophagi show (especially the one from Archanes in Hall 13, and still has a ring on one finger), dead persons were placed in sarcophagi with their arms and legs folded, before rigor mortis set in.

All sarcophagi are decorated to some degree with paintings related to the worship of both the gods and the dead. Motifs included schematic flowers, bull's heads, sacred horns, animals, birds, fish, chariots, ships etc. The scenes attract our interest with their successful drawing, movement, delicacy and sensitivity.

From the 14th century BC on, Minoan sarcophagi, which were initially oval or in the form of chests (cists), took on the cist form almost exclusively, with short legs and a cover, in accordance with the model of the wooden storage chests used in Minoan houses at that time, which appear also to have been used for the burial of the dead. And finally, there are not a few instances of earthenware tubs being used as sarcophagi. Their exterior was usually richly adorned with decorative designs, and their interior covered with depictions of fish or other denizens of the marine world.

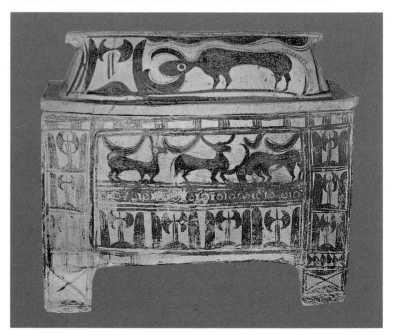

Earthenware sarcophagus with a representation of wild goats and double axes (1450-1200 BC, Archaeological Museum of Hania).

The sarcophagus of Ayia Triada

Anyone who has seen these other Minoan sarcophagi but who has not yet encountered that of Ayia Triada cannot possibly conceive what a very special monument it is. A valuable find from an otherwise insignificant grave in the region, it is the only stone sarcophagus to have been found in Crete; it is covered entirely with stucco and is believed to have contained the body of a prince in about 1400 BC.

Lavish chromatic decoration with rosettes, spirals and bands flanks the main scene, which is in the form of a frieze that unfolds around its four sides and depicts the entire formal rite for burying distinguished dead persons.

On one long side, there is a scene in which a bull is sacrificed. The animal has already had its throat cut and is lying on the altar. Its blood is being collected in a special vessel, and below, two wild goats are waiting their turn to be sacrificed. A courtier accompanies the sacrifice with music and a woman touches the sacrificial carcass in a ritual manner, while another woman offers fruit from a basket on a nearby altar.

The altar is near the sacred tree which is in the sacred precinct. Over it the sacred horns have been placed, where the deity is indicated in the form of a black bird.

 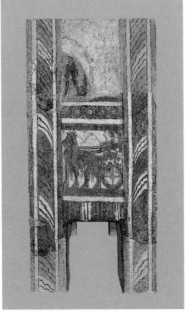

The narrow sides of the sarcophagus of Ayia Triada.

Left: Representation of a chariot carrying two goddesses and pulled by winged griffins over which a bird is flying.

Right: Chariot being drawn by wild goats and a procession of men (1400 BC, Archaeological Museum of Herakleio).

The other long side presents a scene divided into two parts. A woman wearing magnificent garments and a crown is carrying two vessels supported by a horizontal board; she is followed by a lyre player dressed in what look like women's garments. Between two columns that support double axes, there is a vessel into which a second female figure is pouring the libation contents of another jar. This may be the blood of the bull.

The other half of the scene portrays three men dressed in sheepskin offering animals and a little boat to a strange figure without arms or legs, also dressed in sheepskin. The strange figure, which appears to be rising up from the ground, seems to be the dead person to whom the gifts are addressed. Behind him is the sarcophagus or a small temple.

The scene, as experts argue, is certainly associated with religious rites for spring, as suggested by the tree, the branch and the foliage surrounding the double axes.

On one narrow side, a chariot is being drawn by griffins and driven by two female figures towards whom a bird is flying. On the other narrow side there are two successive scenes in two bands, like metopes. On the upper one is a chariot being drawn by wild goats with curved horns and below is a procession of men.

The ordinary viewer is impressed by this work of art that was created to alleviate the pain of death, if it is ever possible

to do so. It shows the "outer forms" of care for the beloved dead person. To the experienced eye of the expert, however, these scenes contain an entire theology. One could also say a great deal by analysing each of the figures, the objects they are holding etc., such as the boat in the hand of one of the male figures, which may possibly be linked with the Minoans' faith in their own paradise, beyond the sea, the Isle of the Blessed, as one might have said in other eras. In any event, we know that entire real boats were placed in many Egyptian tombs, especially royal ones, for the dead person's voyage...

But speaking of graves and the dead, this would be an appropriate point to mention the royal tomb of the Isopati, near Knossos, which has been dated to the 15th cent. BC. What made it unique and remarkable was a hoard of stone vessels imported from Egypt as a kind of "collection of artefacts". Obviously the dead person had close ties with Egypt, as indicated by the fact that the tomb itself, which was hewn entirely out of the rock, presents architectural features which, strangely enough, are highly reminiscent of certain graves contemporary with the oldest of the unguent jars *(alabastra)* it contained. One of these unguent jars, which radiates an astonishing luminance, bears an inscription in two vertical columns that mentions the name and titles of Hatshepsut (1490-1436 BC).

The long sides of the sarcophagus of Ayia Triada.

To the left, the sacrifice of an ox is represented, accompanied by the music of a flute, and to the right a libation accompanied by a lyre and offerings to the dead (1400 BC, Archaeological Museum of Herakleio).

Minoan Script

Sir Arthur Evans distinguished three types of script used by the Mycenaeans: Hieroglyphic, Linear A and Linear B.

Hieroglyphic inscriptions, which preceded Linear A chronologically, are usually found on sealstones, seal imprints, and rarely incised on clay; it is thought that they should be dated not earlier than 1900-1700 BC. Hieroglyphics scholars believe that the script encountered in Crete is quite unrelated to and entirely uninfluenced by the hieroglyphics of Egypt. The hope is expressed that some day a text, perhaps bilingual, will be found in Egypt that will help to decipher Linear A.

The Phaistos Disc was discovered in 1908 in the first Phaistos palace and has been dated to about 1700 BC. Made of baked clay, it is 16 cm in diameter and 12 mm thick. It bears an inscription in a language contemporary with Linear A Script and is unique in that nothing like it has ever been found.

This inscription is the first "printed" text in the world, since each mark was made using a seal impressed on the raw clay.

The fact that none of the seal marks and no analogous text have been identified has led specialists to the view that the Disc was imported from somewhere else.

The two sides of the Phaistos Disc (c. 1600 BC, Archaeological Museum of Herakleio).

The script on the Disc is read from right to left, and therefore from the outside inward. The beginning of the "text" is signified by a vertical line with well-defined relief "teeth" on it, and consists of forty-five different marks, some of which are repeated. Some of the marks that have been impressed on the Disc are, according to the specialists, foreign to Minoan art, such as those depicting a helmet with tufted crest, a woman in unusual dress and a mark slightly reminiscent of a sarcophagus.

Linear A Script is encountered on clay tablets scratched with stone or metal, and are far fewer in number than the tablets bearing Linear B that have been found to date. Tablets with Linear A have come mainly from the villa at Ayia Triada near Phaistos, but a small number of them have also been found in the rest of Crete, and on the islands of Milos and Kea. It is a Minoan script which appeared perhaps in the 18th cent. BC and was used until the mid-15th century BC. It is related to the Linear B Script, but has not yet been deciphered.

During his excavations at Knossos, Evans brought to light some 400 tablets with various symbols incised on them. The script on these plaques was different both from Hieroglyphic and Linear A; he called it Linear B Script, and for a long time retained for himself the right to decipher them, which he either did not have time for or failed to do.

Tablets of this type were not discovered in the Mycenaean centres on mainland Greece until 1939. That year, when Blegen began his excavations in search of the palace of Nestor at Pylos, he very soon came upon the archive room where he found some 1250 tablets. At that same time, similar objects were found in Thebes and Mycenae, so that the overall picture is fuller because these texts are written in the same Linear B Script as those of Knossos.

It is characteristic that tablets of this type have come down to us because they were found on sites that had been destroyed by fire, and were preserved because they were baked. An indeterminate number of them may have been lost forever because they got wet and turned to mud.

Clay tablet incised with Linear A script (c. 1600 BC, Archaeological Museum of Herakleio).

It is also characteristic that while many scholars were engaged in deciphering Linear B, the man who finally succeeded in doing so was a British architect named Michael Ventris, who had also served as an RAF cryptographer, and worked with Cambridge Classics Professor John Chadwick. In 1953 they published their theory that the language in which the Linear B tablets was written was Greek. More recent finds and the comparative study of the theory have proved that they had deciphered it correctly and that the language of the Mycenaean period was certainly Greek, and indeed much older than anything we already knew, including the Homeric works and inscriptions from the 8th cent. BC.

The Linear B texts are mainly inventories of the king's property, "a way of extending the rulers' collective memory," as Chadwick observed, and have been dated between 1450-1375 BC, i.e. the last phase of the Neopalatial period.

More specifically, in terms of their uses, it appears that the hieroglyphic script rarely played a decorative role and was more frequently used for administrative or accounting purposes, as was the case with Linear A. This fact gives rise to questions relating to what the experts tell us was the simultaneous use of the two scripts; that is whether the Hieroglyphic and Linear A scripts constitute the written expression of one or more languages.

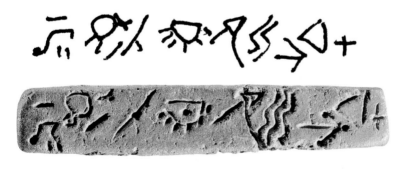

Clay rods with marks of hieroglyphic script and ideograms from Knossos and Mallia (19th-18th cent. BC, Archaeological Museum of Herakleio).

Reconstruction of the palace of Knossos.

Minoan Palaces

- ◆ The palace of Knossos

- ◆ The palace of Phaistos

- ◆ The villa of Ayia Triada

- ◆ The palace of Mallia

- ◆ The palace of Zakros

- ◆ The palace of Archanes

The Customs House and the North Entrance to the palace of Knossos.

Chapter 3

Minoan Palaces

The palace of Knossos

"We ascended to the upper floor, short fat columns painted black and purple were everywhere; we saw flowers, shields and bulls painted on the walls of the corridors. We reached the high terraces, and saw the calm, sunny landscape spread out around us, and against the background of the sky, was Youchtas, the recumbent head of Zeus. The Palace, half-ruined, half-restored, sparkled after thousands of years and the male sun of Crete rejoiced again. You don't see in this Palace the balanced, geometric architecture of Greece; here the imagination, grace and the free play of man's creative power prevail. This Palace grew and spread out in time like a living organism, like a tree, it did not come into being at once, with a pre-designed, certain plan, but kept being supplemented, playing and adapting to the renewed needs of the time. Here man was not led by rigid, unsmiling reason; the mind was useful, but merely a servant, not the master; the master was another..."

From *Report to Greco,* Chapter 6
by Nikos Kazantzakis

Opposite page:
Above:
the reconstructed
West bastion
of the Corridor
of the North
Entrance and,
below: view of
the south House.

Knossos, seat of King Minos, son of Europa and Zeus, was built not far from present-day Herakleio on the road heading toward the interior of the island. In the Odyssey, Homer says of Knossos, the oldest city in Europe in terms of its much-sung power and wealth, that it is very powerful in Crete.

The name of the city is pre-Hellenic, and there are many tales associated with Minos and his brothers. The hill on which the palace was built – and what was by the standards of the times the large city around it – was called Kephala in modern times. It was the first large urban centre in Europe, an unwalled city that spread out as far as the sea around its palace, which was about 4 km from the coast, and must have been inhabited by some 100,000 people.

The name Knossos was retained for at least fifteen hundred years after the palace was destroyed, new structures were not built on the site, nor were there any habitation layers other than Minoan ones. It appears, in any event, that the Greek and Roman city of Knossos did not include the Kephala hill within its limits but probably extended north of it.

The fact that this site was never re-inhabited can be proved not only by the lack of more recent buildings or deposits, but also by the total lack of potsherds from subsequent years. Enormous cypress trees began to grow up around the site thus creating a sacred forest that was dedicated to the primeval goddess of the place, Rhea or Cybele.

During the Hellenistic period, Knossos regained its primacy in Crete and flourished until the period of Roman rule. Then it was destroyed by Gortyn, despite which its name was not lost, and indeed up to the 5th cent. AD it was a bishopric.

As the centuries passed, the name Knossos gradually fell into oblivion, and it was not until 1961 that the village of Makrys Toichos (Long Wall), which had come into being near the site of the ancient city, was renamed Knossos. The Minoan palace – whose most significant parts are those one can see today – was built on the foundations and mound left by another large structure, an older palace, built in about 2000 BC. This, too, had been founded on the remains of a previous settlement, this time from the Neolithic period. In

fact, on Kephala hill the mound from the Neolithic period is about 6.43 m. high, a metre higher than the deposits
from all the previous strata, making it the thickest Neolithic settlement mound in Europe.

It is characteristic that the orientation of the old palace
was retained on the second, more recent one. The major
axis of the Central Court has a north-south orientation.
At the same time there is a second court, the west one.
The difference between these two courts is the fact that
the central one was certainly rectangular in shape, while
the west one may not necessarily have had a specific shape.
In about 1700 BC, a devastating earthquake destroyed not
only Knossos but also all the settlements on central and
eastern Crete, including the palaces of Phaistos, Mallia, Zakros and Archanes. Thus ended a major cultural period on
Crete; at the same time, though, a new period was dawn-
ing, the Neopalatial age, the most brilliant of all the cul-
tures on the island.

On the site of old palaces, larger and more luxurious
ones were built. People's lives then evolved in such a way as
to gather the citizens in the region of each palace around
the monarch. This fact was much more marked and impressive in Knossos. A general mobilisation appears to have
taken place among the people who contributed to building and decorating their king's palace. This second palace at Knossos covers 22,000 m^2, together with its courts,
but without its annexes, i.e. an area double that of the city
of Dimini in Thessaly. We are dealing here with a monument that is unique not to Crete alone, but more generally,
since if we take the palace of Nebuchadnezzar in Babylon
as an example, even though it is precisely double the area
of Knossos, it has five courts and is built on one floor. At
Knossos, there are more storeys: three in the west wing,
and four or perhaps five in the east wing where the royal
apartments are situated.

Today, at a time when large cities are dealing desper-
ately with a variety of ecological problems, the site selected
for the palace and the way it developed appear even more
significant. The hill has steep slopes on the east, north and
south sides. This is why the building was constructed on
more than one artificial level, according to the demands of
the site. In this way the impression created by the palace was

even more magnificent, the view it offered its inhabitants broader, its lighting abundant and its ventilation complete. The various apartments were laid out around the four sides of a central court. This was the residence of the king and his family, the garrison and their servants; here were the storage areas, workshops, administration chambers and religious areas; here, too, official ceremonies, public receptions, council meetings and artistic events were held. In other words, the palace was not merely the king's lavish dwelling; it was a centre with a multiple nature, a basic component of its complex form. It was a building with many floors and an enormous number of rooms, small and large, with courts, corridors, porticos, stairways, characteristic columns, storage areas and workshops. Certainly the visitor unaccustomed to such a sight would be likely to form the impression of a formidable place – chaotic, complex and, in a word, labyrinthine, in the accepted sense of the word today.

When the legend of the Minotaur, the Labyrinth, Minos and the other names associated with this myth came into being, the palace of Knossos had fallen into ruin. But among these "ancient ruins" that retained the grandeur of its area, the memory of its greatness, the scenes of bulls on some walls, and depictions of human casualties in hazardous contests with bulls that were also painted on the walls contributed to creating the myth of Theseus who went with 14 Athenian youths to the palace of Minos and, with the help of Ariadne, destroyed the Minotaur that lived in the Labyrinth.

There was much discussion about the Labyrinth even in antiquity, and many opinions and doubts about its existence, form and position. It was hypothesised that the Labyrinth was the rock quarry at Gortyn, in whose galleries those who were doomed to toil there died. But there is an explicit mention of Knossos. Other theories were put forward too from time to time; the answer to all these is very simple, in contrast to the form of the palace, and was provided by the excavations: the palace of Knossos was at once the residence of King Minos and the Labyrinth.

On 23 March 1900, when Arthur Evans first started digging on Kephala hill, it was already known as the site of a Bronze Age palace. During the period between September 1878 and February 1879, Minos Kalokairinos, an antiquarian merchant from Herakleio, had conducted test excava-

Sir Arthur Evans, contemplating the stone rhyton in the shape of a bull's head, from Knossos.

tions at twelve points on the main site of the West Wing and having kept several of the pots he had unearthed, he studied them at home, wrote about them and had discussions with experts.

A Turkish bey had likewise done some digging in the southeast corner of the palace, in the west storerooms, and north of them in the region of the royal apartments of the king and queen.

In 1881, W.J. Stillman visited Knossos and later gave a paper at the Archaeological Institute of America about the ancient walls and large beams of dressed stone incised with symbols.

What neither Evans nor Schliemann, who had come together with Dörpfeld to Crete in 1886, nor any of the others who had in the past thought about conducting excavations at Knossos had grasped was the vast area of this palace. They believed it covered the space occupied by the West Wing alone. So Evans began excavating on the southeast corner of this wing and moved northwards. When the visitor today sees the extent of the ruins, he can feel this dramatic, unique moment when the British archaeologist realised in amazement that the palace was very much larger than he had realised and that what he regarded as the "East Court" was in fact the Central Court and that the building continued beyond it.

Of Evans's colleagues, we should refer here to Hogarth and Mackenzie, to Fyfe, Doll and the Cypriot foreman Grigoris Antoniou, his successor Manolis Akoumianakis, Pendelbury, the Guillerons father and son, Newton, Piet de Jong, Wace and others. A large number of workers ensured the excavations a very rapid pace – even by today's standards – and at the end of 1902, the palace had been almost entirely brought to light.

1. Sir Arthur Evans (in the white suit) and his colleagues Mackenzie and Fyfe, during the restoration of the Grand Staircase of the palace (Courtesy of the Ashmolean Museum in Oxford).

2. The Throne Room as it was found in the excavations.

3. The South Corridor and entrance to the Central Court.

4. The storerooms.

Sir Arthur Evans continued his work there until 1932. Later, members of the British Archaeological School worked in the region. From 1955-60 there was N. Platon; and from 1957 to 1987 at various points was Hood; and from 1957-1960 and 1976-1970 John Evans worked on the Neolithic remains on the palace site. Other British and Greek archaeologists also contributed.

It should be noted among the little-known facts of history is that Sir Arthur Evans, director of the Ashmolean Museum in Oxford, came to Crete for the first time in 1894 and died in 1941 at the age of 90 in England.

Just before he died, Crete fell into the hands of German parachutists who set up their headquarters in the Villa Ariadne that Evans had built for himself in 1906 southeast of the palace. The villa was later transferred to the British Archaeological School and in 1955 devolved to the Hellenic State.

A major issue associated with the excavations and the restoration of the palace at Knossos concerns the restorations carried out by Evans. From the outset of the works it was clear that the gypsum rock, a material susceptible to weather changes, required that large sections of the building be roofed.

Later, as there was more than one floor, many of the architectural members had to be placed in the position and on the floor from which they came. However, the manner and the materials used to this end were strongly criticised, since they were said to have brought about the ostentatious restoration of the structure, thus altering its character, since some sections remained with the colours of the past and others acquired a "modern" façade.

Non-specialist visitors are unlikely to spend much time worrying about the experts' criticisms of the restorations, but will be delighted and astonished with what they see and what they imagine as they move around the palace of Minos.

The "Rhyton bearer",
a figure from the wall
painting of the procession
in the Propylaeum
(1600-1400 BC,
Archaeological Museum
of Herakleio).

Opposite:
The archaeological site
of Knossos. Aerial photograph.

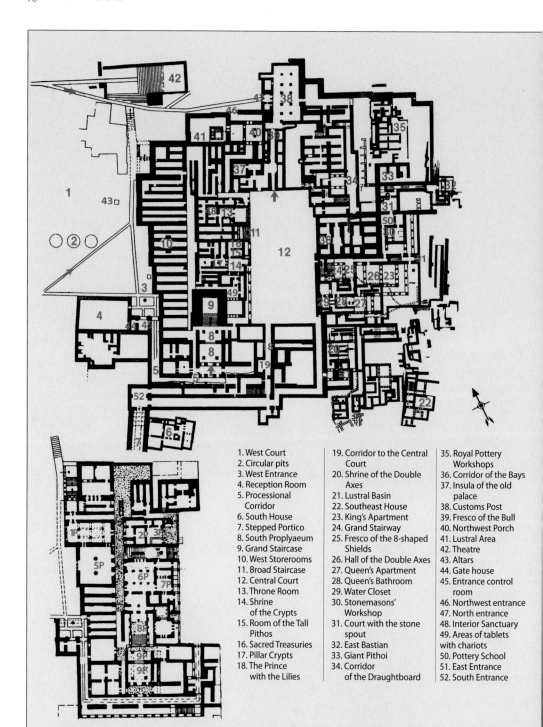

1. West Court
2. Circular pits
3. West Entrance
4. Reception Room
5. Processional Corridor
6. South House
7. Stepped Portico
8. South Proplyaeum
9. Grand Staircase
10. West Storerooms
11. Broad Staircase
12. Central Court
13. Throne Room
14. Shrine of the Crypts
15. Room of the Tall Pithos
16. Sacred Treasuries
17. Pillar Crypts
18. The Prince with the Lilies

19. Corridor to the Central Court
20. Shrine of the Double Axes
21. Lustral Basin
22. Southeast House
23. King's Apartment
24. Grand Stairway
25. Fresco of the 8-shaped Shields
26. Hall of the Double Axes
27. Queen's Apartment
28. Queen's Bathroom
29. Water Closet
30. Stonemasons' Workshop
31. Court with the stone spout
32. East Bastian
33. Giant Pithoi
34. Corridor of the Draughtboard

35. Royal Pottery Workshops
36. Corridor of the Bays
37. Insula of the old palace
38. Customs Post
39. Fresco of the Bull
40. Northwest Porch
41. Lustral Area
42. Theatre
43. Altars
44. Gate house
45. Entrance control room
46. Northwest entrance
47. North entrance
48. Interior Sanctuary
49. Areas of tablets with chariots
50. Pottery School
51. East Entrance
52. South Entrance

Piano Nobile (Upper floor)

1P. Sanctuary room
2P. Area with rooms
3P. Antechamber to the Throne Room

4P. Corridor of the Storerooms
5P. Large Hall
6P. Hall with Tricolumnar shrine

7P. Broad Stairs
8P. Grand Staircase
9P. South Propylaeum

The map on page 70 will be helpful in orienting us on our tour of the archaeological site of Knossos. The numbering of the site will help visitors find their way around, as the numbers correspond to those on the diagram.

We enter the archaeological site of the palace by the West Court (**1**), where the upward-sloping corridors and the altar bases indicate that this must have been the starting-point for processions.

On our right is a bust of Evans, the reconstructor of Knossos. On our left are three Circular Pits (**2**), as much as five metres deep; vestiges can be seen of the houses which were built on this site before the palace and were later used as granaries or as dumps for the remains of sacrifices. This latter view is supported by the ceremonial implements and animal bones found there.

We enter the palace proper via the West Entrance (**3**). On the stone base which has survived was a wooden column. This is followed by the guard-house and a Reception Room (**4**), in which there was a throne.

We continue along the narrow Processional Corridor (**5**), in a southerly direction. The corridor takes its name from the frescoes which were found there, showing a procession of hundreds of young men and women, almost life size, bringing offerings to the gods.

At one time, the corridor, which ran in parallel to the western facade of the Palace, turned to the east and ended in the Central Court. Today it is not possible to follow it for all its length and for that reason we leave it at an earlier point to proceed through the door on our left and head for the South Propylaeum (**8**).

Façade
of one section
of the West Wing
from the West Court.

East façade
of the West Wing.
The stairs led to
the first floor and
to the Central Court.
In the reconstruction,
part of the
Propylaeum,
the Tricolumnar
Shrine (upper floor)
and the Throne
Room complex can
be seen.

Southwest of the Processional Corridor, on the edge of the Palace, can be seen the remains of the South House (**6**). This was built in about 1600 BC, after the destructive earthquake, in the vicinity of the Stepped Portico (**7**), which lies to its west, and must have been the property of a nobleman.

A little below the stream we can see the foundations of a bridge built in the Early Palace period, which linked the Stepped Portico to the Caravanserai. This building was used as a purification or lustral area: it had running water and baths where visitors entering the palace on this side could wash before presenting themselves before the priest-king.

A long paved road began here, and led to the southern coast of the island; along it, commercial traffic set out for Egypt and the East. In the Caravan-serai was found the famous "fresco of the partridges and hoopoes", a copy of which has been installed in its original position. The southern façade of the palace was crowned by sacred double horns.

1. Copy of the wall painting of the Procession in the South Propylaeum.

2. The large South Propylaeum.

3. View of the Piano Nobile (upper floor). In the background is Mt Youchtas.

Now we enter through the imposing Propylaeum (**8**), on which were frescoes of a procession of young men carrying vessels. Here too was found the famous "Cup Bearer" (priest-king). What we see on the walls of Knossos is a copy, the original of which is in the Herakleio Museum today.

We continue to the Grand Staircase (**9**), which was flanked by colonnades and led to the upper floor, the Piano Nobile, where the official apartments were. The Grand Staircase had been completely destroyed by earthquakes and was restored by the archaeologists. At the head of the staircase we pass through an entrance with an ante-chamber and then into the Tricolumnar Hall, where the procession of young men may have ended. To the south was the Treasury; its items of value and the gifts brought to the Sanctuary had fallen through on to the ground floor, where they were found (**1P**).

The Piano Nobile is bisected by the open-air Long Corridor (**4P**), which provided light to the rooms on either side of it. After the Corridor, on the left, is the Large Hall (**5P**), of the two columns and a smaller one with six columns, which may have been a shrine. From here we can see the ground-floor storerooms, where many enormous earthen-ware stor-

2

3

age jars for wine, olive oil, grain and honey were found. The total number of jars found in the palace storerooms was about 400, with a total capa-city of 78,000 kilos; there were 21 storerooms, of which three, on the southern edge of the palace, were no longer in use. The most important finds produced from this area of the palace, however, were the piles of clay tablets in Linear B script, containing inventories of the palace fittings and products, together with the names of the men and women who lived there. It seems that this Great Hall must have been the palace accounting department; the tablets had fallen through to the ground floor. There used to be a wooden staircase that led into the Long Corridor of the storerooms, which unlike the Piano Nobile corridor, was quite dark. When the staircase burned down it was not replaced.

We now enter the Hall of the Frescoes, which is above the Throne Room **(13)** and communicates with it by a circui-

tous staircase. This hall contains a series of copies of frescoes found in the palace and in a neighbouring house. Here we can admire the "Blue Ladies" and the scene from the bull-leaping from the east wing of the Palace, as well as the "Saffron gatherer" and the "Miniature Frescoes" from the cell area, the "Leader of the Blacks" from the House of Frescoes and a whole series of representations of the plant and animal kingdom.

On the south side of the Hall of the Frescoes, at right angles to the Long Corridor, a Broad Staircase **(11)** leads down to the Central Court. The traces of more steps on our left testify to the fact that the palace had a third floor at this point. The

Storerooms on the ground floor of the West Wing. There are rows of large jars (*pithoi*) beside the walls and, on the floor in the middle, a row of stone containers known as chests.

paved Central Court **(12)**, measuring 50 x 20 m., separates the official state chambers on the west side from the private apartments on the east. As in all the Minoan palaces, it is the nucleus of the whole complex. It was here that religious ceremonies, athletic performances and contests, and other activities took place. In addition, it provided light and fresh air for the surrounding rooms.

On the western side of the Central Court, under the Hall of the Frescoes, was the Throne Room **(13)** set amid a group of rooms dating from the Late Minoan period. The Throne

Room consists of an antechamber with stone benches (blackened by the fire that destroyed Knossos) and a wooden throne which is a copy of that in the Throne Room itself. Here the archaeologists have placed a large porphyry vessel.

We now come to Throne Room proper, which is protected by a wooden railing. Against the north wall is Minos' alabaster throne; griffins, symbols of power, are painted on the walls to the right and left. Directly opposite the throne is a small Lustral Area. After the Throne Room is a small Shrine with a high bench on which cult objects were found. Next to

1. Throne Room (Reconstruction by K. Iliakis).

2. The antechamber of the Throne Room.
The porphyry basin was placed here by Evans. Against the north wall is a wooden copy of the throne between stone benches.

this is a room equipped with a kind of grill which, it is believed, was a Kitchen.

South of this group of buildings was the Palace Shrine. One of the Miniature Frescoes shows the layout of this area. A few steps lead down to the Shrine of the Crypts **(14)**, an open area, beyond which is the Room of the Tall Pithos **(15)** and then the Treasuries of the shrine, where the superb faience snake-goddess was found. To the west of the lobby are two rooms with square pillars in their centre, with the double axe carved on them. These are the Pillar Crypts **(17)**, which are believed to have been of a sacred nature. To the north of the first Crypt is the Channel Room, where the blood of sacrificial animals was collected.

From the Lobby, a double door opened onto a dark corridor leading to a number of storerooms. The three last storerooms to the south belong to the Old Palace. From here, a narrow staircase leads up to an open area - the only part of the Palace to have been used in subsequent centuries, as the Hellenic temple which stood here testifies. In the southwest corner of the Central Court, where the processional corridor ends, is a copy of the famous relief fresco called "The Prince of the Lilies" **(18)** in its original position. The fresco shows an idealised Minoan royal figure.

From the South Entrance **(52)**, beneath which in Early Minoan times was an underground guard room hewn out of the rock, a corridor led eastward to the small Shrine of the Double Axes. This is an austere little structure dating from the Late Minoan period. To the south of it there was a lustral area, together with the remains of a staircase and a light-well. From here, the Corridor of the Sword Tablets led north to the Queen's apartments; the corridor took its name from the clay tablets excavated there. Beneath the southeastern corner of the Palace are the ruins of houses from the Middle Minoan period. In the House of the Sacred Podium, which borders on the other two, there was a raised platform of honour. A narrow corridor may have led to a staircase to the Central Court. From here, one descends to the Southeast House **(22)**, with its pillared crypt and an altar for sacrifices.

The east wing of the Palace stood on a hill, and at some points it must have been five floors in height. This wing is dominated by the Grand Staircase **(24)**, with its broad, low steps, one of the greatest works of ancient architecture.

One of the giant pithoi with relief medallions.

It begins about halfway along the eastern side of the Central Court and divides the east wing into its northern section, where the Palace's storerooms and workshops were located, and its southeastern section, where the royal apartments were. We climb the Grand Staircase, with its light-shaft and the columns which lined it, an outstanding example of Minoan engineering. On the east wall of the veranda on the first floor of the Upper Portico has been placed a copy of the Fresco of the Eight-Shaped Shields (**25**).

The miniature wall painting of the Tripartite Shrine.

The balcony of the royal garrison, with a copy of the wall painting of the eight-shaped shields.

On the ground floor was the main Hall of the Colonnades. The light-well supplied the rooms with light and fresh air. Though a door in the northeast side of the Hall of the Colonnades we enter a corridor and turn right, coming to the Hall of the Double Axes (**26**), so-called because of the frequency with which this motif is repeated on the walls. To the left is the Outer Chamber of the Double Axes, where a wooden throne now occupies the place of the original. To the east and south of this hall there were colonnades and light-shafts.

We leave the inner hall through the south door, and after passing along a crooked corridor reach the Queen's Megaron (**27**). Over the entrance is a copy of the splendid Dolphin Fresco.

On the northwest side of this hall is a small room with a bath and a fluted column, the Queen's Bathroom (**28**). To the

The Hall of Double Axes. Restored, with a wooden copy of the throne.

southwest is the Corridor of the Painted Pithos, which ends at a Water Closet (**29**). Light comes from an open area called the Court of the Distaffs because of the symbols carved on its flagstones. In the eastern wall is an advanced drainage network, details of which can be seen in the dark corridor which follows, left of the Bath toward the Central Court.

After this corridor, on the right, is another dark room: the Dungeon, which may have been a treasury. This room produced a large clay tablet with lists of names, next to each of which was ideogram showing whether they were men or women. We continue along the corridor, coming to a staircase, on the left, which leads to the upper floors. Under this stair was found the ivory bull-leaper statuette.

The corridor brings us back to the Hall of the Colonnades, from which we continue through the Hall of the Double Axes (26) and turn left into the East Portico of the Palace. Behind this is a hall with a pillared square, the Stonemasons' Workshop (30), where pieces of Spartan basalt were found that were in the process of being worked. Then comes the School of Pottery (50), with benches and basins. North of this is the open-air Court of the Stone Spout (31), which look its name from the spout which drained the rainwater from the roof of the Great East Hall.

To the east is the East Bastion (32) with the interesting East Entrance (51) that has a complex system which automatically checks the force of the rainwater as it runs down. Farther north of the Court of the Stone Spout are the Magazines of the Giant Pithoi (33), remnants of the Old Palace.

We continue along the paved Corridor of the Draughtboard (34) where an inlaid gaming-board similar to a chess board was found. Under the railing can be seen the clay pipes from the aqueduct of the Old Palace.

To the west of this corridor is the North West Hall and to the northeast are the Royal Pottery Workshops (35), in which the incredibly delicate 'eggshell' ware of the Middle Minoan period was found. Southeast of the Corridor of the Draughtboard there is an open court with the upper part of the drain which ended in the Court of the Stone Spout. From here a doorway to the west leads to the Corridor of the Bays (36) whose massive pillars show that there must have been a large hall on the upper floor.

1. Painted reproduction of the Queen's Apartment (Drawing by Piet de Jong).

2. Painted reproduction of the draughtboard, a royal game.

1. Exterior view of the Hall of the Double Axes.

2. North Lustral Basin.

3. Upper floor of the Hall of the Double Axes.

4. The Theatral Area.

5. View of the grand staircase.

We continue, reaching the Upper Portico and, on the left, the Upper Hall of the Double Axes.

The door to the southwest leads to the Upper Queen's Megaron. The floor-plan here is exactly the same as on the ground floor. To the south, a narrow corridor where the vases with the lilies were found leads to two rooms which today have been covered. Behind these rooms, the Corridor of the Sword Tablets leads off to the little Shrine of the Double Axes.

We return to the Central Court (12) and head north, going into the North Entrance Corridor. To the east of this were storerooms, while to the west are the foundations of the oldest part of the Palace, the so-called Old Cells (37). When the New Palace was built, these rooms were buried beneath its floor. It was above this area that the Saffron Gatherer and the Miniature Frescoes were found.

The corridor ends in a pillared chamber, the so-called Customs Post (38), to the east of which is the Northeast Entrance Corridor. Initially, the North Entrance was the same width as the Customs Post but in later times the fear of invasion caused the Minoans to narrow it to the width of this corridor and build bastions on either side. Above the bastions are porticoes with friezes in relief.

The western portico, which has been restored, was chosen as the site for the modern copy of the wonderfully lifelike fresco of the Charging Bull (39) shown against the background of an olive grove. To the west of these porticos is the North-

west portico **(40)**, followed by an Antechamber and the Lustral Area **(41)**, where those entering the Palace from this side could be purified.

As we leave the Palace to the northwest, we come to the Theatral Area **(42)**. To the west of the Theatre is a road heading north for the Little Palace.

From the Little Palace, continuing north, we can visit the Royal Villa which lies to the northeast in the valley behind Knossos.

1. Section of the relief Wall Painting of the Bull.

2. Painted representation of the Wall Painting of the Bull charging through an olive grove.

3. The West Portico with the restored Wall Painting of the Bull, and in the background the North Lustration Basin.

4. The House of the Sacred Rostrum.

5. Restored light well of the upper floor of the West Wing, with copies of frescoes from the House of Frescoes.

6. View of the North Lustral Basin.

3

4

6

5

The Palace of Phaistos

"…besides, the city was disturbed with superstitious fears
and strange appearances, and the priests declared that their
sacrifices intimated some villainies and pollutions that were
to be expiated. Upon this, they sent for Epimenides the Phaestian
from Crete, who is counted the seventh wise man by those that
will not admit Periander into the number. He seems to have been
thought a favourite of heaven, possessed of knowledge in all
the supernatural and ritual parts of religion… When he came to
Athens, and grew acquainted with Solon, he served him in many
instances, and prepared the way for his legislation… Epimenides,
being much honoured, and receiving from the city rich offers of
large gifts and privileges, requested but one branch of the sacred
olive, and, on that being granted, returned."

(Plutarch, *Life of Solon*,
translated by John Dryden)

The visitor's initial impression of Phaistos is quite different from that of Knossos. First of all, the approach to the
site is completely different. The visitor travels several kms in-
land from Herakleio, through a lush, verdant landscape, and
finds himself looking towards the west side of Mesara, the
largest, most productive plain on Crete. The hill of Phaistos
is seen as the first in a series of low hills that extends from
east to west in between Mt. Ida (Psiloritis) and the Asterou-
sia range, overlooking the abundant plain and its outlet to
the sea. On top of the hill are the remains of the palace of
Phaistos, a site as important as that of Knossos and of no
less significance either architecturally or in size. It is obviously contemporary with the palace of Knossos, as there are
similarities in the style of construction, the use of materials
and the layout, and it seems possible that they may have had
the same architect or that the one palace might have served
as a model for the other. The palace of Phaistos falls short of
Knossos only in terms of its interior decoration because despite the fact that the walls are plastered with lime, they bear
no painted scenes. Also very few objects were found here.

With its wonderful view, which for the Minoan ruler also
meant control over the region, its pleasant climate and the
abundant water from the Lethaios river, today's Geropota-

mos, Phaistos was one of Minos' three major cities, as noted by Diodorus and Strabo, although it was more closely associated with Rhadamanthys and his son, Phaistos, who gave the place his name. In Book II of the *Iliad*, Homer called the city "a joy to live in" (Book II, line 743); Plutarch referred to it as the homeland of Epimenides. Initially independent in historical times, it minted a large number of coins, some of which bore representations of Europa on the bull, while others depicted Hermes, Herakles etc. In the 3rd century BC, it came into conflict with neighbouring Gortyn, which ultimately destroyed it. Its final documented destruction was in the 2nd century BC.

A British ship's captain named H. Spratt identified the site on which Phaistos stood in the mid-19th century. Fr. Halbherr and his associate An. Taramalli began excavations in 1884. The palace and a part of the city were unearthed after 1898 by the Italian Archaeological School of Athens under Halbherr and L. Pernier (1900-1917). Halbherr mainly excavated and studied the older stages of the palace on the southwest side and parts of the city from Minoan times lying west of the palace at Ayia Fotini and Halara.

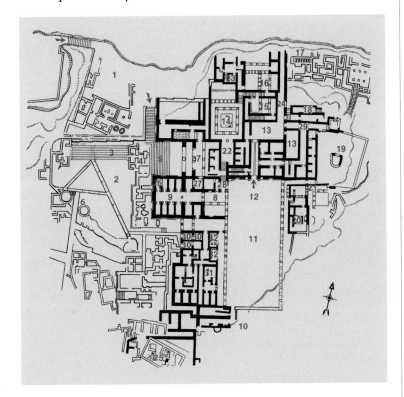

1. Northwest Square
2. West Court
3. Theatral Area
4. Shrine in the Old Palace
5. Propylaeum stairs
6. Circular pits
7. Propylaeum
8. Antechamber to the Storerooms
9. Corridor to the Storerooms
10. South Entrance
11. Central Court
12. North Entrance to the Royal Apartments
13. Court of the North Wing
14. Peristyle
15. Queen's Apartment
16. King's Apartment
17. Room in which the Phaistos Disc was found
18. Purification Basin
19. East Court with kiln
20. Lustral Basin
21. Portico
22. Area in front of the Peristyle
23. Cistern
24. Corridor
25. Temple of Rhea
26. Storeroom with pithoi
27. Lustral Basin room
28. Stairs to upper floor
29. Corridor to East Court
30. West Court Shrine
31. Room with the Pillars
32. Rooms with benches

Apart from the fact that walking around Phaistos, you have the feeling of being on an acropolis, the picture of the archaeological site is entirely different from that of Knossos, because here restorations were limited to what was absolutely necessary in order to stabilise some weak walls and to cover some very fragile sections with concrete or plastic roofing, as they were in danger of being lost forever if exposed to the elements.

The palace of Phaistos, an enormous trapezoidally-shaped structure, occupies the greater part of the hilltop and, owing to the contour of the terrain, was built on four different levels from south to north.

The large Central Court was not located precisely in the centre but slightly to the east, which is why the west wing of the palace is larger than the east. Indeed, part of the east wing, the southeast quarter in particular, disappeared when the land subsided due to erosion.

The paved Central Court (**11**) measures 55x25 metres and has porticos on its two long sides. There are corridors on

The palace of Phaistos. art of the West Court, the sanctuary of the old palace and the stairs to the Propylaeum.

all sides of the palace that either begin or end in the Central Court, where the inhabitants would gather, especially in the cool porticos, to rest, converse or exercise. In the northwest corner there is a stepped constructed base made of large dressed stones that might testify to the existence of an altar in antiquity. Two large rectangular panels with small columns placed in a row above them – perhaps tables for offerings – seem to corroborate this view. Dedicatory offerings of oxen were also found here. Two rooms in the west wing open onto the west portico (**30**) of the Central Court; they contain benches faced with plaques of gypsum decorated with fluting. Given the layout of the rooms next to them and the finds unearthed there (libation cups, figurines, small altars), these rooms are believed to have been used for religious purposes.

The West Court (**2**), as it exists today, dates to the Protopalatial period, that is, to the first palace built on the site. It is paved and is an inestimable monument as it is regarded as the site of the "oldest theatre in the world" because of the layout of its northeast corner.

This part of the court is in the form of a magnificent stairway comprising eight broad steps at the top of which is a retaining wall, which means that the stairway did not provide access to some upper level, but was rather a structure intended for many people to sit on so that they could watch religious and other rites, processions and games. The fact that religious services were held there can be confirmed by the existence of a shrine on the east end of the stairway, which comprised four rooms, the largest of which was the sanctuary itself. It, too, had been part of the earlier palace and was preserved with respect as a sacred place. This court is crossed by a "processional way" which starts out from the Propylaeum (**7**), the main entrance to the palace, that had a column in the middle.

The paved processional way went in the direction of the retaining wall where the "King's Box" may have been, while another branch headed westward. South of this fork are four round constructions known as "circular pits" (**6**) *(kouloures)* which are thought to be have been either cisterns or granaries.

From the west court, a magnificent flight of steps leads to the Propylaeum, a superb creation of pre-Hellenic architecture. It is a building belonging to the New Palace and is situated on

Amphora from the archaeological site of Phaistos (17th-15th cent. BC, Archaeological Museum of Herakleio).

the northeast corner of the west court. A stairway 14 metres wide (5) leads to a broad landing, also part of the Propylaeum (7), which consists of a large porch to the west and a portico to the east with a dividing wall in which is the main door of a double entrance, all magnificently laid out. Further down there is a smaller entrance leading to the corridor that separates the storerooms in the north from the complex of rooms in the south that are considered by scholars to be a group of sanctuaries.

Between this corridor and the Propylaeum there is another corridor (9) leading from the Central Court to the Store Rooms, five on each side. The corridor is covered by a roof that is supported in the middle by a square pillar. Large storage jars both intact and broken and containing traces of cereals and fruit were found in the storerooms. Only the ground floor survives, but there must have been an upper floor. The size and significance of the Phaistos storerooms cannot be compared to those of Knossos. Despite the enormous, fertile expanses of the Mesara plain, the ruler of Phaistos was not as wealthy as the ruler of Knossos.

To the north of the central court are the Royal Apartments (15, 16) which are built on a higher elevation and command a spectacular view of Mt Ida.

A paved corridor (12) with a duct running down the middle leads to a small, closed courtyard (13), also paved, from which another corridor leads north to the entrance of the royal quarters, yet another unique masterpiece of Minoan architecture. It contains corridors, stairways, many doors, light wells, chambers, purification basins, wall paintings and floors that are paved at several points with alabaster. It is a lavish building divided into the "King's Megaron" (16) to the north and the "Queen's Megaron" (15), which is somewhat smaller, to the south. It is believed that there was an upper storey here as well.

To the east of the royal apartments, on a lower level, a complex of buildings has been preserved that was part of the Old Palace, but continued to be used later. The easternmost chamber in this complex was named the "Potter's Storeroom" because many unused vessels were found here, one inside the other. The room directly to the west, with a peristyle of pillars and columns that opened to the north, is believed to have been a private residence. Some believed that this next room to the west was a kitchen, others a sanctuary.

The most important room of all is the fourth (17), because this is where the famous Phaistos Disc was found. To-

gether with the Disc, a tablet inscribed with Linear A script was found. L. Pernier, the archaeologist who excavated the site, maintained that this room was the Palace Archives that were in fact situated on the upper floor of the building.

On the Phaistos Palace site, in addition to findings from the Protopalatial and Neopalatial periods, remains were also found of the Neolithic and Prepalatial periods. After the palace was destroyed in about the mid-15th century BC by the eruption of the Thera volcano, which is regarded as having destroyed the other Minoan centres too, the site was abandoned and just a few sections seem to have been used, obviously by private citizens in the late Minoan years. A fairly significant settlement developed in the Protogeometric and Geometric periods. The sanctuary of Rhea or the Great Mother (25) with a small temple in the middle was built in the early Archaic period, very near the palace and to the south.

The palace of Phaistos touches one in a strange and evocative way. Upon leaving part of it, the visitor soon wishes to return. Its lucid architecture creates the odd sensation in visitors that that they have missed something and makes them want to return to confirm this feeling. There are fascinating,

1. View of the palace.

2. Sculpted figure of pregnant woman. From the palace of Phaistos (19th-18th cent. BC, Archaeological Museum of Herakleio).

eloquent details, such as the polished alabaster floor tiles in the Queen's Apartments, the well-made storage jars in the storerooms, the atmospheric staircase in the west court, the small sanctuaries, the crystal clear atmosphere, the landscape that can be glimpsed through the branches and foliage of the trees, the base of a column in one room and the large expanse of the areas that seem to isolate one section from the others and from the other floors. All of this evokes a gran-

deur and mystery that is revealed gradually, as though some invisible hand were guiding you to the exit, but you don't really want to leave, because nature and the ruins have generously provided you such a memorable experience.

Before we leave Phaistos, mention must be made of many superb examples of Kamares ware that were found in the Old Palace and constitute a collection of particular interest at the Herakleio Museum.

1. Storeroom with pithoi.

2. The Central Court.

3. Ruins of the temple of Apollo.

4. Section with houses.

5. Panoramic view of the palace of Phaistos.

The Villa of Ayia Triada

The Villa of Ayia Triada is inextricably linked to the Palace of Phaistos for many reasons.

Ayia Triada is located on the south coast of Crete near the Minoan Palace of Phaistos. A "villa" came to light there: a large complex of buildings that is believed to have been the summer residence of the kings of Phaistos, as well as a highly significant financial, administrative and religious centre with an independent organisation.

The name Ayia Triada (Holy Trinity in Greek) was taken from a small 4th-century church on the site, since the ancient name of the site has not been preserved. The site was excavated in the early 20th century by the Italian archaeologist L. Pernier. The palace of Ayia Triada was built in ca. 1550 BC and was destroyed by fire in 1450 BC. It was later inhabited in the Classical era, at which time it was used for the worship of Zeus Belchanos.

The villa of Ayia Triada is divided into two sections: the area of the settlement (1) in the northeast, and the area of the

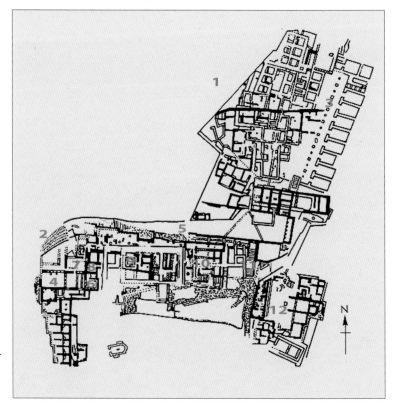

1. Settlement
2. Main Villa
3. Agora
4. Antechamber
5. North Ramp
6. Room with benches
7. Archive room
8. Storerooms
9. Room with central pillar
10. Royal Apartments
11. Stairs to the North Ramp
12. East Wing.

Main Villa (2) in the southwest. The settlement is made up mainly of small houses which, as can be concluded from the finds of little value, obviously belonged to the people working in the complex, artisans or farmers, while in the east was the Agora (3) a large oblong area with a portico and shops. The settlement is separated from the Main Villa by the so-called North Ramp (5) which used to lead to the villa entrance by a stairway to the upper floor which has not been preserved. In the area of the Main Villa of Ayia Triada, there were wall paintings in small rooms of a religious nature. The extant fragments depict a female figure among plants, another female figure beside sacred horns, a procession reminiscent of a scene from the sarcophagus of Ayia Triada, a representation of wild cats stalking birds (the best preserved) and a marine landscape.

1. Wall painting from the villa of Ayia Triada (17th-15th cent. BC, Archaeological Museum of Herakleio).

2. View of the NW apartments of the villa.

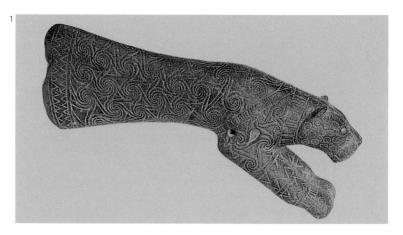

Palace of Mallia

In 1915 the Ephor of Antiquities discovered on the north coast of Crete, about 40 kilometres east of Herakleio, the third most important Minoan palace in a region with highly developed tourism and the intensive cultivation of bananas. It is similar to the Palace of Phaistos in terms of its size (8,000 m² approximately) but inferior in terms of the materials used to build it.

The first person to discover antiquities in the area was the British Captain Spratt in the 18th century. He attempted to plunder the site, but during the digging, one of the workers was crushed by a mound of earth and the effort was abandoned.

Later, the accidental discovery of ancient artefacts led Iosiph Hatzidakis to begin excavations which lasted for many years and led to the discovery of a significant part of the west wing of the Mallia Palace.

Lack of funds prevented Hatzidakis from continuing. Excavations were taken up by the French Archaeological School from 1921 to 1932 under F. Chapouthier, J. Charbonneau, R. Joly and P. Demargne.

The system applied by Evans, with its impressive but controversial restorations, was not followed at Mallia, Phaistos or the other palaces; in recent years however enormous, especially designed roofs have been erected over certain parts of the monument at Mallia in order to protect it.

The site is entirely different from that of the other Cretan palaces, because as one looks northward, the sea extends as far as the eye can see, and the view to the south is dominated

1. Royal sceptre of slate in the form of a panther from the palace of Mallia (c. 1650 BC, Archaeological Museum of Herakleio).

2. Panoramic view of the palace of Mallia.

by Mt Diktys and the Lasithi plateau, whose old-time inhabitants have now moved to the richer coasts.

There is no irregularity or outcropping of the terrain here, so that the apartments in the palace are clearly outlined over the flat land that appears to have given the region its present name, which is Omalos (=regular), from which Omalia and Mallia are also derived. The prehistoric name of the site is not known.

Legend tells us that Sarpedon, brother of Minos and Rhadamanthys, was driven away from Knossos together with his friend Miletus, who is regarded as the founder of the city of the same name in Asia Minor. The name Miletus is likewise associated with that of the village just beyond present-day Mallia, which is called Milatos (and became known in modern history for the incident in 1823 in which the inhabitants of the region sought refuge from the Turks in a large nearby cave and after a 15-day siege were all slaughtered). This may have been Sarpedon's kingdom.

Regarding its form, the palace of Mallia presents the same basic features as the other palaces, with a large central court, sanctuaries, craft workshops, etc.

Very few traces of the Prepalatial Period remain here, and the findings from the Neolithic age are meagre. Here too,

2

two construction stages can be seen: the first from the Protopalatial period (c. 1900 BC) and the second from the Neopalatial (1650 BC). The palace at Mallia was destroyed, as were all the others, in 1450 BC by the same cause. In the past, the absence of Kamares ware here provoked discussions as to whether this palace may have been abandoned for a time and rebuilt later. But this absence eventually proved to have been due to the fact that the potter's craft was at a lower level here, since Mallia was generally a provincial palace with objects of lesser quality than those of Knossos or Phaistos. Even the construction materials were inferior. Black limestone was mainly used on the thresholds, while the external walls were built of sand mortar and limestone. Bricks made of mud and seaweed were used on the interior walls which became solid matter in the fire that destroyed the palace and presented a formidable obstacle to the early excavators. The columns were of wood.

The original entrance was on the south side, but today the visitor approaches the site from the west, where the paved West Court (1) is crossed from north to south by a Processional Way whose south leg forks eastward, forming a triangle. The thickness of the walls testifies to the existence of a second floor.

In the west wing were the Storerooms (19), which communicate by means a north-south corridor. It is believed that the areas to the east of this corridor were used as storage space, since in one of them a large number of vessels for household use were found. Religious areas and the throne room (7) were found in the west wing.

The Throne Room at Mallia is totally different from those at Knossos and Phaistos. The excavators described the area as a loggia (8), i.e. an open gallery with a roof supported by a col-

1. West Court
2. Room with many doors
3. Lustration Basin
4. Hypostyle Shrine
5. Oblique Structure
6. Hypostyle Hall
7. Throne Room
8. Loggia
9. Central Court
10. Altar
11. East Storerooms
12. Southeast Entrance
13. South Entrance
14. Area in which the kernos was found
15. Grand Stairway
16. Antechamber and Pillar Crypt
17. South Wing Shrine
18. Granaries or Cisterns
19. West Storerooms
20. Private Apartments
21. North Entrance
22. Northeast Storerooms

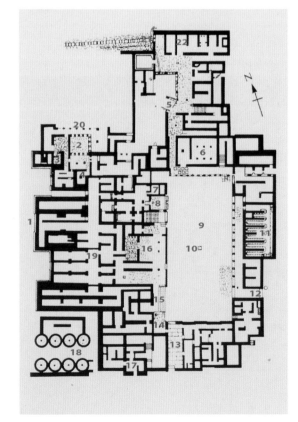

umn, rather like a veranda. This area was on the northwest side of the main court, but elevated above it. It was also accessible from the inside by a stairway on each side of which are traces of a column base. On the floor in front of these stairs, a squared stone juts out that may perhaps be the remains of a throne.

The Throne Room opens onto the Central Court (9) by a broad flight of steps, in the middle of which was the base of the column that supported the roof. The sacredness of this place is proved by the findings from the room that was right behind it and in which were found several valuable and characteristic objects: a stone sceptre with one finial in the shape of an axe and the other in that of a leopard's head, found in a large earthenware jar, a knife and a long sword with a stone handle that had been revetted with gold and fitted with a spherical rock crystal finial containing amethyst-coloured glints.

Directly south of the loggia are the broad stone steps that led to the upper floor and were also used to seat people for court events. Farther south a Sanctuary (16) was discovered, a paved hypostyle crypt in the centre of which were traces of two pillar bases and in front of it, to the east, an antechamber (16) lined with a bench and a two-columned portico, right opposite the site of the Altar (10) in the middle of the Central Court. This part of the Palace at Mallia, 48x23 m., is what remains of the structure of the Protopalatial period. On the east and north sides there were porticos that gave it a grand air. The alternation of square pillars with columns is a characteristic feature of Minoan buildings.

On the south section of the West Wing are broad tiers of stone steps (15) described by experts as a Theatral Area. Near it the "*kernos* of Mallia" (14) was found, a large earthenware offertory vessel 0.90 m. in diameter, with 34 small hollows around a larger one in the middle, an artefact unique of its kind.

A little farther on is the broad paved South Entrance (13) from which a long corridor leads to the central court. On the left of this entrance is a Sanctuary (17) in which a stone altar

1. The Mallia kernos.

2. In the SE corner of the West Court, eight circular pits were built that were either granaries or water storage jars.

stands with hollows on each side and carvings in the shape of a cross and a star. Many significant votive offerings and cult objects were found on this spot.

To the west of the South Entrance there is a section containing eight circular structures with a column in the centre and plastered inside, which are believed to be granaries (**18**). Some clay lamps were found in this area.

The East Storerooms (**11**) basically constitute the east wing of this palace; grains and pulses were kept in some of them, in addition to wine and oil. There are a total of six rooms equipped with low benches on which to place storage jars and a system for collecting liquids that may have been spilt accidentally. At the end of the eastern portico of the Central Court was the southeast entrance to the palace (**12**), which led to the paved roads of the city quarters, in which many houses have been excavated.

There were two courts in the north wing, the Court of the Tower and the North Court, to which the north entrance (**21**) to the Palace of Mallia leads. On the outside it leads to the flagstone-paved road to the port.

Of the many significant apartments in this wing, the most important is the so-called Hypostyle Hall (**6**) behind the north portico of the Central Court; the roof is supported by six pillars that are not symmetrically placed in relation to the walls of the hall. It was regarded by some as a sacred area, and other scholars believed that above it was the Dining Hall.

Between the North Court and the Tower Court, a shrine was built after the final destruction of the palace, perhaps during the Postpalatial years. It has been named the Oblique Structure (**5**) because of its orientation in relation to the other buildings on the site. An earthenware grape-press or

1. The stairway south of the elevated Loggia.

2. Section of the North Entrance, and large pithos with spirals.

3. View of the West Wing of the palace.

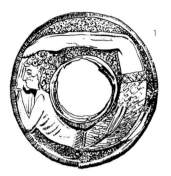

vessel used in making oil was found in a room opposite the Oblique Structure.

On the south side of the Tower Court an apartment was identified with two rooms and the particularly solid walls that gave the court its name. In it were vessels containing pulses. To the west the Royal Apartments (20) were identified, with a paved hall and the only multiple doors (2) in this palace. There was also the Hypostyle Sanctuary (4) in its southern section in which vestiges were found of animal bones and a number of clay tablets, rods and small discs bearing inscriptions in Linear A script. Beside the chamber with the many doors, a purification basin was excavated (3), in its antechamber was found the Sword of the Acrobat, its handle revetted with gold, and one other sword.

In the north part of the North Court, a large storage jar from the Neopalatial period was found decorated with spirals. To the north and east of this court another two storage complexes were found (22).

The careful visitor to the Mallia Palace will observe its large number of storage areas and its small workshops. These are the main characteristics of its rural character and were certainly associated with religion, as is obvious from the many sanctuaries and significant cult objects.

One could not leave the Mallia site without visiting **Chrysolakkos**, the site of the royal cemetery from the Protopalatial period. It was discovered north of the Palace, near the sea, and despite the fact that the cemetery had been looted, it nevertheless yielded many remarkable finds (and to grave robbers from all periods).

This was a group of tombs with a complex layout within an area of 39x50 m. Apart from *kernoi* and an altar, the famous gold jewel was discovered here that depicts two facing bees holding a honeycomb between them. This is an object of superb artistry with granular decoration, one of the most exquisite examples of Minoan gold work and of its art more generally.

1. Line drawing of the gold disc on the Mallia sword (1700 BC, Archaeological Museum of Herakleio).

2. Stone triton with incised and relief decoration from the palace of Mallia (18th-15th cent. BC, Archaeological Museum of Ayios Nikolaos).

The Palace of Zakros

The excavations begun by Professor Nikolaos Platon in the little settlement of Kato Zakros in 1961 brought to light the fourth palace in Crete, which is much smaller than that of Knossos. It has an area of 8000 m² and was built on a particularly magnificent location near the sea, on a leeward cove on the island's east coast.

The singularity of the site, both because of its safe harbour and its great importance in maintaining contacts between the Cretans and the peoples of the East, particularly the Egyptians, was the main reason for building the palace at this point. It is believed that the Minoan Cretans must have used the port of Zakros as a naval base. We do not know what the ancient name of the region was.

The excavation works that began in the early 20th century under British archaeologist D.G. Hogarth unearthed twelve houses on the hills surrounding the town that descend to a small but highly fertile valley owing to the large amount of water in the region. These houses, most of which have been dated to the Protopalatial period, probably belonged to officials, had more than one floor and their ground floor had no external stairway.

Two construction phases have been recorded. The first was c. 1900 BC, but very few traces of it have been preserved; the second phase is dated to about 1600 BC. The palace at Zakros has all the main features of the other palaces contemporary with it, all of which were destroyed in about 1450 BC by the same cause.

After their destruction, however, one main difference has appeared. Whereas the inhabitants of the other Minoan palaces had time to take all their valuables with them when they left, in Zakros, a great many treasures remained in situ. Moreover, the palace of Zakros was preserved unlooted. The fact that life did not continue on this site and that no subsequent settlements were

1. Central Court
2. Altar
3. Reception Room
4. Ceremonial Room
5. Symposium Chamber
6. Main Shrine
7. Lustration Basin
8. Treasury of the Shrine
9. Archive Room
10. Workshop Complex
11. Queen's Room
12. Cistern Room
13. Fountain
14. Basin – Lustration Bath
15. Cookhouse – Dining room
16. Storerooms

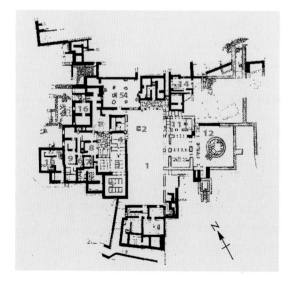

built on the ruins contributed to preserving superb works of art and to ensuring better understanding of the Minoans' way of life, government, religion and art.

Walking up the paved road from the port and up its northeast side through a stepped corridor and a small court, the visitor would have reached the Central Court (1). This Court, with an area of 30x12 m, differs somewhat from the orientation of the other palaces, facing in a NE to SW direction. In the NW corner an altar had been built (2).

In the west wing were the religious areas as well as the storerooms and workshops. A carefully designed Reception Hall (3), its main section paved with earthenware tiles, led to the Ceremonial Hall (4), which was also accessible directly from the court. Here two stone libation vessels of superb artistry were found, one in the shape of a bull's head and the other a stone rhyton depicting a mountain top sanctuary. On this site a number bronze implements were likewise found, among which were saws 1.7 m. long that were operated by two people simultaneously. The floors were constructed in a characteristic way by being covered with stucco over which various designs and joints were drawn. To the south was the Symposium Hall (5).

To the west of these apartments was a sanctuary consisting of a total of eleven rooms of different dimensions. The main Sanctuary (6) occupied the centre of this wing. It was a small room with a high bench along one side for various cult-related objects to be placed on, and another, lower one, on the opposite side. Next to it, a basin was discovered for religious purification (or "lustration") (7) with eight steps leading to it.

In this part of the palace, another two areas present special interest. The first is the Sanctuary Treasury (8), the only one that had not been looted in all of Minoan Crete; it yielded important finds including a rhyton of rock crystal in 300 pieces which were re-assembled and joined together. On the north side the Archive (9) was discovered, in which

Libation rhyton of chlorite bearing the relief representation of a mountain top sanctuary (c. 1500 BC, Archaeological Museum of Herakleio).

small clay tablets inscribed with Linear A Script were found in small boxes. Thirteen of them were burned during the fire that destroyed the palace, i.e. they were baked and thus preserved accidentally.

In the area around the sanctuary rooms, six large bronze talents were found in the shape of double axes, each of which weighed some 30 kg. Bronze was imported from Cyprus in this form. Also in the same area, three intact elephant tusks were discovered that probably originated in Syria. These latter findings were obviously on the upper floor, where the workshops must have been located. Somewhat later there must also have been workshops and perhaps also a dyer's shop in a building outside the west wall of the palace (**10**).

The apartments of the king and queen (**11**) came to light in the east wing, which the experts say must have been related to rituals, as testified or suggested by a spacious structure with a circular tank below the ground with steps leading into it and waterproof walls, in which spring waters were collected. This tank may have been a ritual area, although many other hypotheses have also been expressed as to its function. The excavating archaeologist described the area as the Chamber of the Basin (**12**) and regarded it as a Throne Room. It was certainly a unique structure in Minoan chronicles and may perhaps suggest some Egyptian influence. There were "sacred lakes" in Egyptian temples that were used as ritual baths. The royal quarters were located on the upper floor.

1. View of the north section of the palace where the "makeshift" dining room was found, in direct relation with the "official" one on the upper floor.

2. The Central Court.

3. Panoramic view of the archaeological site of Zakros.

In an apartment farther south in the east wing, another spring was found, the waters from which were channelled into a constructed fountain (13). The excavator related it to the "fountain made by human hand" mentioned by Homer. Fourteen steps descended to its floor. A cup was found there containing olives, a unique find, because the olives had been preserved until that moment, by an accident of nature, as though they had just been cut from the tree. Another basin-lustration bath (14) was discovered in the northeast apartments with traces of stucco that preserved wall paintings with sacred themes.

In the north section of the palace a hall 12x12 m. can be discerned to the west, which must, according to the archaeologists, have been a cookhouse and makeshift dining room directly related to the official dining room (15) on the upper floor. Beside it were two areas full of cooking utensils.

In the south section of the palace were the workshops, in which rock crystal, ivory and other materials were employed,

and possibly a workshop for preparing fragrances.

All over the site there were light wells, many doors, windows and a remarkable drainage system, which has been preserved in good condition in the first court in the northeast part, where the road up from the sea ended. Farther up, in Traostalo and in the "Gorge of the Dead", many prehistoric graves were discovered. Even today, the Zakros palace district is fertile, with abundant waters and a beautiful beach on the sea facing the East, its waves bearing whispers of ships from Syria, Palestine and Egypt, loaded with riches and ideas. More practical modern tourists, who arrive in their cars, will find charming little tavernas with raki and delicious Cretan mezédes.

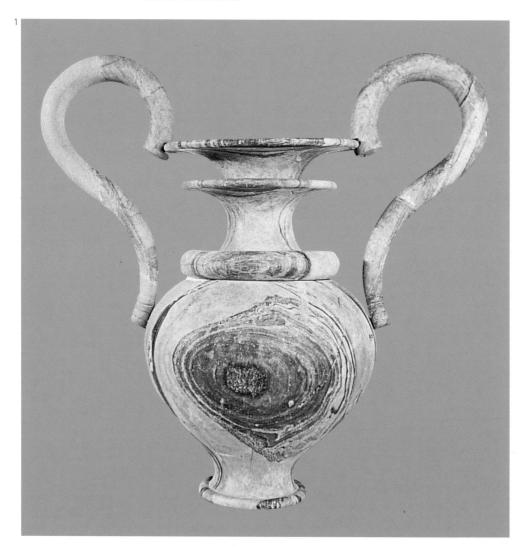

The Palace of Archanes

The first to speak of the importance of Archanes, about 15 km. southeast of Herakleio, was Stephanos Xanthoudidis in 1912. Later, Evans described the ruins found at various points in the modern settlement as palatial, expressing the view that they belonged to a summer palace. In 1964 Giannis Sakellarakis started digging there and continued from 1966 on within the context of the excavations conducted by the Archaeological Society with the collaboration of Efi Sapouna-Sakellaraki.

The work continues up to the present day with great success, and has brought to light yet another palace in Crete.

1. Ritual amphora of multicoloured marble, from the Lustration Basin of Zakros (1550-1500 BC, Archaeological Museum of Herakleio).

2. Earthenware figurine of a female figure sitting on a horse, from Archanes (1350-1100 BC, Archaeological Museum of Herakleio).

Also, in 1964 a Minoan cemetery was discovered nearby Fourni, which today constitutes one of the most important archaeological sites in all of Crete. In 1979 the first independent Minoan temple in Crete was discovered on this site, in which, according to Sakellarakis, human sacrifices were conducted.

The central core of the palace building at Archanes discovered by Giannis Sakellarakis was situated in the centre of the modern city a fact that, owing to construction, makes it impossible to reveal the monument as a whole, which according to the archaeologist had the same area as the other known palaces. Explorations took place at four points and yielded findings that argued for the existence of a palace. This is the Tourkogeitonia site, which comprises the core of the palace, the area of the cistern alongside and northwest of Tourkogeitonia, the Theatral Area and the Archives. Excavations at these points, the first two of which constitute a city block, while the others are located farther south, are fairly extensive and being supplemented continually.

The palace complex of Archanes was first built in about 1900 BC on top of Prepalatial ruins. Habitation, with minor changes, continued on the same site even after the disaster of 1450 BC, during the Mycenaean, Geometric and subsequent periods, up to the years of Turkish rule and into modern times. The Minoan settlement was built around the palace.

According to Sakellarakis, the archaeologist who conducted the excavations, in terms of materials and mode of construction, the Palace building is comparable only with those of Knossos and Phaistos. The walls have been preserved at certain points up to a height of 2 metres and the external walls sometimes exceed 1 m. in thickness. In the eastern section of Court 1 a pile of stones has been left as it fell during the disaster. A little to the north, a grand entrance with two columns has been preserved, parts of which are complete enough to measure their diameter. Between the east column and the door posts are four two-hollow altars that have been placed in such a way as to form a square table, each side of which is 0.96 m long, indicating the existence of a sanctuary related to the entrance gate.

In the adjacent Antechamber are the remains of a wall painting, perhaps a woman holding a branch. To the north there is a large square (Area 3) which, as testified by the finds, was of some importance and very carefully built, as were the floors above it. Here 43 loom weights and ten flywheels of semi-precious stone came to light.

To the north is Area 4 which, according to the archaeologist, is the most remarkable point in this section of the excavation; it had at least two floors and stucco on the walls which must have been decorated; on its western section there was a low bench on which to place objects, and in its northeast corner a stepped pedestal.

In this area many pots were found of various sizes and two large clay tubs, one of which was decorated with spirals and the other with beautiful plant, especially palm-type, motifs. The lid for one of them was also found. Ivory artefacts, a large piece of red jasper and other objects were likewise unearthed. The marked signs of an intense fire are obviously due to the fact that wood beams and other wooden objects were gathered at this point.

This section continues in Corridor 5, which is closed on the north side by a wall in which there are two doors. The east door leads to an area in which two elaborate porphyry lamps were found. One of them is decorated with a relief spiral and the other with finely worked leaves, splendid examples of Minoan miniature sculpture.

Corridors, porticos, steps, stairwells, and auxiliary areas were accessible from the west door of Corridor 5. In one of them many more loom weights were found, indicating the existence of textile workshops with looms on the upper floors.

A particularly official chamber is Hall 10, along whose north, east and west walls ran a built bench and in the middle of the floor was a square of bluish marble tiles. Here too, there were probably two upper floors. The second floor at this point must certainly have included a sanctuary, as argued by the rich finds that had fallen to the lower floor, such as an offerings table, sacred horns, the clay base of a double axe, animal figurines and potsherds. This hall had one door that communicated with Court 11 and another on the west, in the area under the neighbouring building.

Court 11 is a continuation of Court 1, but is interrupted by the existence of an alcove with benches *(exedra)* on the north section of which is a rectangular poros stone altar with a small trapezoidal altar on its narrow west side. A stone duct that is directly related to the exedra altar crosses Court 11.

In the area of the exedra, about 30 conic cups without handles were discovered, among other things. In the adjoining Area 13, which must have had a second floor with a lavish apartment, more than one hundred pots were found, most of which were amphorae, although there were also boiling pots, conic and round cups. The duct from Court 11 crosses Area 15, which appears to have been open-air.

Area 17 was named the "Sanctuary of the Elephant Figurines", and was regarded by the excavator as being particularly important, with three floors, multicoloured stucco and rich finds that attest to religious usage. Among these finds was a gold and ivory group consisting of six figures, of which two heads and parts of arms, legs, etc. have been found. Near one of the two poros stone bases for double axes, a hoard of pots was found of various sizes in the marine style, uniformly decorated with octopuses, nautiluses etc. One part of this area was destroyed by the construction of a building in the later Mycenaean period. The exploration of further sections of the palace is proceeding at a slow pace, since it is hindered by the neighbouring buildings. What has become obvious from the excavations is that the building was destroyed by a terrible fire, that much of it had been built with luxury materials, that strongly religious elements and structures are present and that it holds great surprises for the excavators of the future.

North of Area 18, which is west of Area 17, a Minoan aqueduct was identified in 1922 by Evans and brought to light in 1964 by Giannis Sakellarakis. Although this aqueduct is today under a road and a house, it contributes to the study of the water supply systems in the early Minoan period. The cistern belongs to the Palace Building, and during the Neopalatial period it was decorated with flowerpots and appears to have been associated with some religious function, as can be concluded from the figurines (bell- and animal-shaped) that were found here. When the Palace was destroyed, the aqueduct also collapsed, as indicated by the presence of a rare find, a human skull.

Not far from the palace area described above, a paved Theatral Area was discovered to the southeast that was traversed by four "walkways", as they were described by the excavator. The eastern one is double and at one point forms an angle with another. On the southwest side there is a ditch. Above the ditch and the sidewalk stands a stepped altar, together with sacred horns on which a branch was carved. Also found here were some conic cups on a large slab. All these are regarded as characteristic of an area used for ceremonies of a theatrical and religious nature, as testified by the features of analogous structures in other Minoan palaces.

Southwest of the Palace, on the site of the Kalpadakis building, tablets were discovered bearing Linear A script, one of which was written on both sides. The area was designated an Archive, and is valued for its finds. The building remains were not significant. The finds include a clay replica of a Minoan house, which provides us with significant information in the study of Minoan architecture.

After the final destruction of the Archarnes Palace, life there seems to have continued throughout the Mycenaean period with remarkable prosperity, as indicated in particular at Fourni, where its cemetery was discovered, a site of exceptional importance for the entire island.

A visit to what has so far been discovered of the palace of Acharnes provides factual evidence of the often insurmountable difficulties of conducting archaeological exploration. At the same time strange feelings are created, because as one

Earthenware replica of a stone-built house from Archanes (c. 1600 BC, Archaeological Museum of Herakleio).

observes the experts working silently and systematically, a bit farther down a car may drive by, or a baby may cry. Then the air is filled with the aroma of home cooking. This means that, however distant the remains of the Palace of Archanes are chronologically from the modern surroundings in which life has continued for some 3500 years, the proximity of the two gives them another dimension, it makes them more familiar, witnesses to the continuity of history that is woven into an eternal canvas despite the forces of nature and human indifference. The nightmarish power of earthquakes is characteristic, visible in the thick and well-built wall of the building which it moved several cms horizontally over the floor of the structure.

Stairway and rooms along the South Wing at Fourni.

Gournia, view of the agora area
and the ruins of the workshops.

Other sites

- ◆ The Cemetery at Fourni
- ◆ Minoan Cities
- ◆ Minoan Villas

The Cemetery at Fourni

Fourni is the name of a small hill between Upper and Lower Archanes, northwest of Youchta. In 1964 Giannis Sakellarakis excavated a chamber tomb on the eastern slopes of the hill and in the following year brought to light two vaulted tombs.

The excavations have progressed since then to reveal an entire necropolis which was originally in use in about 2400 BC and continued for about 1300 years until the late 11th century BC. There are hundreds of interments, including tombs of distinguished persons such as kings, and the data yielded by the study of the finds has provided information not only about burial customs, religious and social life and art, but also about the Cretans' relations with Cycladic merchants and other Mediterranean peoples.

The area excavated so far covers 2 hectares and has been landscaped as an archaeological park. According to the excavating archaeologist, it constitutes one of the most important cemeteries in the Cretan-Mycenaean world and the most significant in Crete.

At the northernmost point of the excavated region at Fourni, a rectangular Mycenaean Grave Precinct has come to light that was used throughout the 14th cent. BC. Just one part of this precinct has been preserved. It contained seven rectangular pits over which gravestones (stelae) had been erected in three cases, a virtually unknown custom in Crete. The dead had been placed in the pits in earthenware burial chests (larnakes), just a few pieces of which have survived, perhaps because they were damaged during removal. The number of funeral gifts, their quality and the entire layout of the site testify to the fact that persons of aristocratic origin were buried there, to whom respect and worship were rendered.

South of the Mycenaean Grave Precinct, one of the region's five vaulted tombs came to light in 1965; it had been built in the first half of the 14th cent. BC and its side chamber included the first unlooted royal tomb.

Its style is similar to that of the known vaulted tombs in Mycenae and Orchomenos, and the road leading to its entrance (dromos) is very long compared to others known in Crete.

The area around vaulted Tomb A had already been looted, it would appear, in the Minoan period. At one point near the sealed passage from the tomb to the side chamber, a unique finding was discovered: the skeleton of a horse that had been sacrificed in honour of the dead person in the chamber, and cut into pieces. Among the rocks in the partition, the skull of a bull was discovered that constituted a significant factor in understanding problems of a religious nature. Inside the chamber, there was nothing but a large larnax which, judging from its content, is regarded as certain to have contained the body of a woman, a princess or a queen, and indeed a woman who had held priestly office, as attested by the sacrifices and representations of religious symbols (eight-shaped shields, sacred horns and sacred knots).

One of the most impressive finds was a lavishly decorated footstool, also unique for Crete, faced on the front with 87 extant pieces of ivory, bearing representations of eight-shaped shields and two handles portraying warriors wearing helmets.

Vaulted Tomb B is considered the most important structure discovered so far in the Fourni cemetery. It represents six different chronological periods and is surrounded by miscellaneous areas – a total of twelve – comprising an enormous complex with a rectangular external form. The vaulted tomb in the centre of the complex is the highest structure, above ground; it must have been built before 2000 BC and used for some six hundred years (until the first half of the 14th cent. BC) for the burial and possibly worship of royal persons, as noted by Sakellarakis. The finds were not particularly enlightening as regards its many years of use.

In a compartment adjoining the tomb, in Area 5, a cist-shaped sarcophagus was found carefully hidden inside walls, and contained

Clay rattle (sistrum) from Mortuary Building 9 (2000-1900 BC, Archaeological Museum of Herakleio).

the remains of at least 19 persons. Because the sarcophagus had been hermetically sealed, their bones which had been carefully laid down, were preserved in excellent condition and in fact some types of human bones were preserved, such as finger bones and sacra, which have never before been found even in intact graves.

Area 6 was preserved in good condition with its covering earth layer undisturbed, and is the most important in this complex. It had a pillar and many interments, and yielded a gold ring depicting a goddess with a griffin, a steatite sealstone in the form of a bull's head, a silver dressing pin bearing a Linear B inscription, and many tiny pieces of stucco indicating the presence of wall paintings. The pieces are miniscule, so that it is impossible to restore any scene, but the colours are discernible. The pillar bears witness to the religious use of the area.

Mortuary Building 6, behind and to the west of vaulted Tomb B, which consists of six long narrow chambers from different periods, is a type of repository, together with an area for interment in the ground, in sarcophagi and in clay burial jars. In the two eastern chambers, 196 skulls were found. Rich and significant funeral gifts came to light in this area among which were 16 sealstones of various shapes and materials. Among them was one with 14 seal surfaces. Some of the sarcophagi bore the marks of incised script, a rare find in Minoan Crete, which suggests trade contacts.

Between Mortuary Building 6 and vaulted Tomb B was found the largest repository in Minoan Crete, in terms of the number and variety of vessels, which was of a cult nature, since it contains no large pots or vessels of household use. On the contrary, vessels of hitherto unknown shapes were found, including some very small ones.

Mortuary Building 3, south of vaulted Tomb B, is square-shaped, well-built and was in use from at least 2000 BC until and perhaps after 1400 BC, but not many people are buried here. Four of them were buried in larnakes (two are children). Its characteristic is the importance of the graves and the many pieces of ivory.

Vaulted Tomb C, the third, is above ground and was discovered south of the vaulted Tomb B complex. It contains a total of 45 interments: in 11 sarcophagi, a large earthenware jar (with the remains of 18 people), and in the ground. Sakel-

Ivory figurine from Vaulted Tomb C (2500-2100 BC, Archaeological Museum of Herakleio).

larakis noted that this was the first time that in a Prepalatial vaulted tomb (its construction dates to about 2250 BC)
there is a confirmed number of burials. Funeral gifts were
not found in the sarcophagi or in the graves in the ground,
but rather under them and in a layer of stones of differ-
ing sizes. The total number of these funeral gifts was 269.
Among them were 15 Cycladic figurines (of various materials) a rare event in a vaulted tomb, as well as a large number
of obsidian blades. The characteristic feature of this vaulted tomb is the existence of a window south of the entrance.

In Mortuary Building 9, which contains a large number
of interments, among the many and significant objects discovered was an earthenware rattle (sistrum) made of very
thin clay, and similar to the one depicted on the "vessel of
the reapers" from the villa at Ayia Triada. It may be the oldest musical instrument to have been found, not in Crete
alone, but in all of Europe.

Mortuary Building 19, the only apsidal Cretan structure
dating from the era between 2100 and 1950 BC, lies to the
south of Mortuary Building 18, has particularly thick walls
and many burials with rich gifts. Farther south vaulted
Tomb E was found, the earliest mortuary structure in the
region, dating to 2400-2300 BC. It was built above ground
and had not been looted. It is characterised by the multi-
tude of sarcophagi and a considerable number of superbly
worked seals of various materials.

Vaulted Tomb D is situated at the southernmost point of
the necropolis and surprised the excavating archaeologist
with the unlooted grave of a woman dating from the first
half of the 14th cent. BC. Part of it was hewn into the rock,
and even though it was not very well preserved, the position of the skeleton was unchanged, as was the arrange-
ment of the grave gifts, among which was jewellery of gold
and various other materials (sard, glass paste, electrum and
faience). Near the skeleton was found, among other things,
a bronze mirror that the dead woman was holding in front
of her face, and a tiny jasper sealstone, perhaps the small-
est ever found.

In the space between vaulted tombs A and B there are
two other structures which, as the excavating archaeologist noted, are unique in terms of their use, not in Minoan
Crete alone, but throughout the entire Aegean.

1. Entrance to Vaulted Tomb A.

2. Vaulted Tomb B

3. The long path to the entrance to Vaulted Tomb B from the east.

Building 21 is underground, drop-shaped, vaulted and has steps by which one can descend into it. It is believed to have been a purification basin, a fact suggested by the lack of graves and by its architectural form, which is interpreted as an addition to the neighbouring vaulted tomb. In other words, this is a structure that served the needs of the living on the cemetery site. It was in use until the 13th cent. BC.

Building 14, completely different in shape and size from Building 21, was regarded by the excavating archaeologist as a structure for the permanent accommodation of the living and at the same time for the manufacture of products required for burials and related practices. It had been built as early as the mid-16th cent. BC and consists of two sections, east and west.

The first section, with two storeys, had a special area for the production of wine, since excavations revealed a wine press, i.e. an earthenware vessel for pressing the grapes, a tank for collecting the must and large jars. Olive pits were found in one of these jars. In the same wing there were looms.

The second section is a large rectangular area which may have been entirely paved. The stone bases of three columns were found, a unique structure for Minoan and other cemeteries, and it appears to have been an outdoor area. Similar structures can be found only in the organised cemeteries of Egypt and under the supervision of priests.

Such a brief description of this enormous and significant cemetery of Minoan Crete can give the reader only a very vague picture. But it does constitute a stimulus for a careful walk in a region that has yielded a great deal of data, the importance of which has not yet been fully appreciated as it is still being studied, and every day new finds come to light.

Minoan Cities

In a protected region with a protected port on Mirabello Gulf on the north shore of Crete, some kilometres east of Ayios Nikolaos, archaeologist Harriet Boyd-Hawes excavated an entire Minoan city early in the 20th century.

Its name is not known, but it is referred to as the "Pompeii of Crete", present-day Gournia, with a "palace" on top of a low hill. It had a central and western court, storerooms, a sanctuary, spiral roads and a small shrine to the Snake Goddess, built after the town was destroyed in 1450 and re-inhabited.

On the east coast of the island, not far from the Toplou Monastery and the Palm Grove of Vai, two km. from the present day village of Palaikastro on the Rousolakkos site, a large and important city was excavated.

The site was first inhabited in about the middle of the 3rd millennium BC. A settlement grew up during the Protopalatial period, was destroyed in the 17th cent. BC and later rebuilt, at which time it covered an area of 50,000 m2. It was destroyed in 1450 BC and reappeared for 150 years between 1350 and 1200 BC. Its location on the east coast – and the resulting easy contact with the countries of the eastern Mediterranean from its natural harbour – was a crucial factor in its development.

1. Gournia

2. Palaikastro

Houses large and small, streets narrow and wide, lavish structures, damages from war and mechanical causes, as well as a gold and ivory half-burned statue of a god, and some examples of wonderful Minoan art are, in summary, the main features of this Minoan city, in which there was a temple of Dictaean Zeus in historical times.

Another Minoan settlement was discovered near the village of Stylos Apokoronou, which may have been related to the Minoan Aptera, and is believed to have been established during the Prepalatial period. A significant find from this settlement was a pottery kiln from the Postpalatial period. Another settlement near Stylos, organised by districts, is currently being excavated at Samonas.

Minoan Villas

At various points on Crete, traces of large buildings have been discovered that are in the form of small palaces with large halls, sanctuaries, purification tanks, rooms with many doors, storerooms, a second storey, workshops etc. It appears that they were dependencies of the palaces and belonged either to the kings themselves or to members of the royal family. We have already discussed the villa at Ayia Triada near Phaistos.

Southwest of Herakleio, Iosif Hatzidakis excavated three monumental residences or small palaces at Tylissos. There were wall paintings in one of them.

Very near Archanes, to the south, on the Piso Livadia site, Spyros Marinatos excavated the villa of Vathypetro in the 1950s, which in his view did not appear ever to have been completed. In addition to everything else, this villa had an olive press and a grape press, a ceramics workshop and kiln.

Near the Palace of Knossos a number of residences were discovered, outstanding among which were the Small Palace and the Royal Villa east of Heraklio at Nirou Hani, etc.

1, 2. Views
of residences, or
small palaces at
Tylissos.

3. Vathypetro.
View of the east side
of the site.

4. View of part
of House A from
Tylissos.

Index

Bibliography

- Alexiou, St. *Μινωικός Πολιτισμός* (Minoan Civilisation), 2nd ed., Herakleio.
- Betancourt, P., *The history of Minoan pottery*, Princeton, 1985.
- Chadwick, J., *Γραμμική Β: Η πρώτη ελληνική γραφή*, Kakoulidis, 1962.
- --- *Γραμμική Β και συγγενικές γραφές*, Papadimas, 1992.
- Evans, A., *The Palace of Minos*, New York, 1964.
- Faure, P., *Η καθημερινή ζωή στην Κρήτη τη Μινωική Εποχή*, Papadimas, 1999.
- Kenna, V., *Cretan Seals*, 1960.
- Levi, S., *Festos et la Civilita Minoica*, v. 5, Roma 1973-1981.
- Marinatos Sp.-Hirmer, M., *Η Κρήτη και η μυκηναϊκή Ελλάς*, 1959.
- Marinatos, Sp. *Πρακτικά Αρχαιολογικής Εταιρείας*
  (Proceedings of the Archaeological Society), 1929-1930, 1932-1936 and 1938.
- Nilsson, M.P. *Ιστορία της Αρχαίας Ελληνικής Θρησκείας*, Papadimas, 1999.
- Palmer, L.R., *Mycenaeans and Minoans*, Faber, 1965.
- Panagiotakis, G.I., *Δικταίο Άντρο* (Dictaean Cave), 2nd ed. 1988.
- Papadakis, N.P., *Σητεία* (Sitia) 1989.
- Pendlebury, J., *A Handbook to the Palace of Minos*.
- Platon, N., *Ζάκρος, το νέον μινωικόν ανάκτορον*
  (Zakros: The new Minoan palace) Athens 1974.
- --- *Πρακτικά Αρχαιολογικής Εταιρείας*
  (Proceedings of the Archaeological Society), 1961-1963.
- --- "Crete", Archeologia Mundi, Geneva 1966.
- Sakellarakis, Giannis and Efi, «Ανασκαφή Αρχανών» ("The Excavation of Archanes")
  Πρακτικά Αρχαιολογικής Εταιρείας (Proceedings of the Archaeological Society),
  1966 etc.
- --- Κρήτη *Αρχάνες* (Crete Archanes), Ekdotike Athenon, 1994.
- «Κρήτη-Αίγυπτος, Πολιτισμικοί δεσμοί τριών χιλιετιών»
  (Crete-Egypt, Three Millennia of Cultural Bonds), Catalogue, Herakleio 2000,
  with extensive bibliography.
- *The Dawn of Greek Art*, Ekdotike Athenon, 1994.
- Vassilakis, A., Αρχαιολογικό Μουσείο Ηρακλείου (Archaeological Museum
  of Herakleio), Adam.

Texts: LITSA I. HATZIFOTI
Overall Supervision: DIMITRIS ANANIADIS
Translation: JUDY GIANNAKOPOULOU
Artistic Supervision: EVI DAMIRI
Layout: RANIA TSILOGIANNOPOULOU
Photographs: M. TOUBIS S.A. ARCHIVES
Printing – Binding: M. TOUBIS S.A.